1, 2, 3 JOHN
& JUDE

THE BATTLE FOR LOVE AND TRUTH

DR. DAVID JEREMIAH

Prepared by Peachtree Publishing Services

HarperChristian
Resources

1, 2, 3 John & Jude
Jeremiah Bible Study Series

© 2022 by Dr. David Jeremiah

Requests for information should be addressed to:
HarperChristian Resources, 3900 Sparks Dr. SE, Grand Rapids, Michigan 49546

ISBN 978-0-310-09184-4 (softcover)
ISBN 978-0-310-09185-1 (ebook)

All Scripture quotations are taken from The Holy Bible, New King James Version. Copyright © 1979, 1980, 1982 by Thomas Nelson. All rights reserved.

Any internet addresses (websites, blogs, etc.) and telephone numbers in this study guide are offered as a resource. They are not intended in any way to be or imply an endorsement by HarperChristian Resources, nor does HarperChristian Resources vouch for the content of these sites and numbers for the life of this study guide.

HarperChristian Resources titles may be purchased in bulk for church, business, fundraising, or ministry use. For information, please email ResourceSpecialist@ChurchSource.com.

Produced with the assistance of Peachtree Publishing Services (www.PeachtreePublishingServices. com). Project staff include Christopher D. Hudson and Randy Southern.

The quote from William Barclay in the "Reflecting on the Meaning" section of lesson 2 is taken from William Barclay, *The Letters of John and Jude*, revised edition (Philadelphia, PA: Westminster Press, 1976).

First Printing November 2021 / Printed in the United States of America
24 25 26 27 28 LBC 7 6 5 4 3

CONTENTS

INTRODUCTION TO

The Letters of 1, 2, 3 John and Jude

"*My little children, let us not love in word or in tongue, but in deed and in truth. And by this we know that we are of the truth, and shall assure our hearts before Him*" (1 John 3:18–19). The Christians of the first century were facing a difficult battle. False teachers had emerged in their churches who were spreading a gospel that was contrary to the one proclaimed by Jesus, the disciples, and the early apostles. These teachers were creating strife and divisions within the Christian community. The situation was so distressing to John, the beloved disciple, that he wrote a series of letters to remind the believers of the truths that they had been taught—and to call them to remember that Jesus' greatest command was for them to love God and to love one another. In a similar way, Jude—the half-brother of Jesus—called on believers to remember the truth of the gospel and persevere in the face of these attacks from false teachers.

1 JOHN

Author and Date

The writer of this letter does not identify himself, nor does he indicate his intended audience. However, he frequently refers to his readers as his "children" (see 1 John 2:12, 18, 28) and "beloved" (see 4:1, 7), which implies that he not only had affection for them but also held a degree of pastoral authority over them. In addition, the author establishes that he was an eyewitness to the life of Christ (see 1:1–3), and the vocabulary and style of the letter bears similarities to the Gospel of John. Early church fathers such as Irenaeus (AD 130–202) and Clement of Alexandria (AD 185–215), and Tertullian (AD 150–22) thus held that the writer was the disciple John. The letter was likely written c. AD 90, toward the end of John's life in AD 100.

Background and Setting

While John does not identify his audience, it is apparent that he was writing to a group of churches who looked to him as their patron. A clue to their identity can be found in Revelation 2–3, also believed to be written by John, in which he addressed believers in Ephesus, Smyrna, Pergamos, Thyatira, Sardis, Philadelphia, and Laodicea. It is reasonable to assume that John had these same believers in mind when he wrote this letter. John likely wrote the letter from the isle of Patmos, where he had been exiled, and that his purpose was to warn these churches of false teachers who had infiltrated their congregations and were causing division and strife.

Key Themes

Several key themes are prominent in 1 John. The first is that *believers in Christ must resist any teachings that are contrary to the true gospel*. John wrote this letter to counteract the influence of Gnosticism in the early church. The Gnostics believed that matter is evil, so a good God could not have created the physical world, and taught that Jesus did not have a physical body. John was also confronting Cerinthianism, which held that Jesus was born a man, became divine at His baptism, and then became a man again at His crucifixion. John calls on believers to remember the truths they received about Christ (see 1 John 1:1–4; 2:18–29; 4:1–6; 5:6–21).

A second theme is that *believers in Christ must maintain their fellowship in love*. John goes to great lengths to emphasize the importance of the believers loving one another. He singles out love as a key identifying feature of Christianity and stresses that they are able to love one another because God *first* loved them—even while they were still sinners. If that love for others isn't present, people can legitimately question their faith (see 1 John 1:5–2:17; 3:1–24).

A third theme is that *believers in Christ must strive to walk in righteousness*. John warns his readers that if they profess to be true followers of Christ, their "walk" must match their "talk." It is not enough for them to just *say* that they are following Christ—their *actions* must show also that they are following after Jesus. Believers must avoid a lifestyle of sin, follow Jesus' example in loving others, and resist the temptations of the world (see 1 John 4:1–5:5).

2 John

Author and Date

The writer of this letter refers to himself as "the Elder" (2 John 1:1), a designation that led some church historians (such as Eusebius) to conclude it was not written by John the disciple. However, the similarity of language and subject matter between 1 and 2 John suggests the beloved disciple wrote both, and other early church leaders (such as Irenaeus) stated that he was the author. The vocabulary, structure, and grammar of the letter also bears similarities to the Gospel of John. It was likely written soon after the first letter, around AD 90.

Background and Setting

John addresses his second letter to "the elect lady and her children" (1 John 1:1). This could refer to an actual Christian woman and her children in a church, or it could be a metaphorical reference to a body of believers. The situation for writing the letter rose out of the common practice in the early church of members welcoming traveling ministers into their homes. The problem was that many false teachers were taking advantage of the believers' generosity. So John wrote this letter to urge them not to show hospitality to any perverters of God's truth.

Key Themes

Two key themes are found in 2 John. First, *believers must remain faithful to the teachings of Jesus Christ that they have received.* John calls on believers to *know the truth* and *live in the truth.* He rejoices that many are "walking in truth" and again pleads with the believers to "love one another" (see 2 John 1:1–6). Second, *believers must beware of those who seek to deceive them.* The church was less than one century old when the disciple penned the letters of 1 and 2 John, yet false teachings were already prevalent and rampant in the Christian communities. Once again, John urges believers to practice discernment and reject any teachings that are contrary to the message they received—and to keep on rejecting them until Christ returns. They were not to even allow those who professed such false teachings into their homes (see 2 John 1:7–13).

3 JOHN

Author and Date

The writer of this letter once again identifies himself as "the Elder" (3 John 1:1), so the same questions arise about its author as in 2 John. However, once again, the similarities among the letters—and the testimony of the early church fathers—point to John the disciple as the writer. It may have been written before or after the other two letters, but sometime around AD 90.

Background and Setting

John addresses his third letter to "the beloved Gaius" (2 John 1:1). Evidently, another leader, named Diotrephes, had asserted his power by refusing to allow traveling Christian teachers to minister to the congregation. Even worse, he was punishing any members who showed hospitality to those teachers. John wrote to confront Diotrephes and to commend and encourage Gaius, who was serving the community selflessly and walking in the truth of Christ.

Key Themes

As with 2 John, the letter of 3 John is personal in nature and so brief that little space is given for explicit themes. However, we find that John once again calls *believers in Christ to walk in the truth and remain steadfast in the faith* (see 3 John 1:1–11). The apostle mentions "truth" six times in the fourteen verses of the letter and emphasizes that truth goes hand in hand with steadfastness. John also stresses that *believers in Christ should demonstrate hospitality to those who labor for the gospel* (see verses 9–14). John highlights the ministry of Gaius, a church elder who selflessly welcomed traveling missionaries, but condemns the prideful acts of Diotrephes.

JUDE

Author and Date

The author of this letter identifies himself as "Jude, a bondservant of Jesus Christ" (Jude 1:1). Several men are named "Jude" or "Judas" in the New Testament (both are translations of the same name), but the most likely candidate for authorship is the half-brother of Jesus, who was also the brother of James. Early church leaders such as Clement of Alexandria, Origen (AD 184–253), Athanasius (AD 296–373), and Jerome (AD 342–420), all concurred with this designation. It is possible that Jude was written earlier than 1–3 John, sometime in the AD 60s to 70s.

Background and Setting

Much like John's epistles, the letter of Jude was written to counter false teachings in the church. Jude's statement that "certain men have crept in unnoticed" (Jude 1:4) suggests that the false teachers had infiltrated a particular church or a close group of churches. The fact that Jude was going to write to these believers about their "common salvation" (verse 3), but then switched his topic, testifies to the immediacy of the threat. Scholars have noted similarities between Jude and 2 Peter, suggesting that either Jude or Peter borrowed from the other.

Key Themes

Two key themes are prominent in the short letter of Jude. First, *believers must be engaged in defending the faith.* Not surprisingly, Jude would not allow complacency in the church when believers were under attack. He recognized the enemy's strategy was to creep in unnoticed, so he compelled God's people to remain vigilant so that false teachers would gain no ground in the war for people's souls (see Jude 1:1–4, 20–23). Second, *believers must be engaged in living out the faith.* Jude uses key examples from the Old Testament to illustrate that God does not allow sin to go unpunished. The believers needed to resist the enemy's attacks and look for strength to the One who could keep them from stumbling (see verses 5–15, 24–25).

KEY APPLICATIONS

The letters of 1, 2, 3 John and Jude reveal that we are in a *real* battle against a *real* enemy. Satan, the enemy of our souls, desires to bring division in our fellowship with other believers, and he will use whatever strategies necessary to accomplish that goal. He knows that a *divided* church is a *weak* church. For this reason, we must hold fast to the *truth* of the gospel—as revealed in God's Word—and not be persuaded by any erroneous teachings. At the same time, we must seek to follow Jesus' great command to love one another and do the hard things that requires—including sacrificing our time, convenience, and pride for the sake of others.

THE FULLNESS OF JOY

1 John 1:1–10

GETTING STARTED

What do you most appreciate about your fellowship with other believers?

_____

_____

_____

_____

_____

_____

_____

_____

_____

_____

_____

_____

_____

_____

_____

_____

_____

_____

_____

SETTING THE STAGE

In the opening verses of this letter, the disciple John gives us his "statement of purpose" or motivation for writing it. He states, "That which we have seen and heard we declare to you, that you also may have fellowship with us . . . [and] that your joy may be full" (1 John 1:3–4). John is reminding his readers of the incredibly good news that they have received: *Jesus has saved them from their sins*! They no longer stand condemned before God.

John wants his readers to comprehend the benefits they have received from accepting Jesus as their Savior and becoming born again. He desires for them to experience the full and abundant joy that comes from having a relationship with Almighty God and living in fellowship with other like-minded and hope-filled followers of Jesus. Sadly, the implication is that it is possible to be a Christian . . . but *not* experience this full joy of knowing God.

Perhaps you have encountered such people. Maybe you know those who claim to know Christ and be in fellowship with Him but display no excitement about their faith. They look, sound, and act just like everyone else in the world! These are the people to whom John is writing—those who need to build a foundation of fellowship and joy in their walk with Christ.

There is a natural progression in what John is saying. We have fellowship "with the Father and with His Son Jesus Christ" (verse 3), which means we share in fellowship with all who are in fellowship with God. This unity with God and each other should be the source of the fullness of joy (excitement) in our lives. What is amazing is that John wrote these words while Diocletian was emperor in Rome. Diocletian was a cruel and vicious dictator who despised Christians. Yet in the midst of that atmosphere of persecution, John was telling his readers that they could have *fullness of joy* through fellowship with Christ and each other.

John's words should cause us to examine our own lives. Although we may not face the kind of persecution that the Christians under Diocletian faced, we will still encounter countless circumstances and situations that will threaten to rob us of our joy. We have to be wary of the "joy-killers" and continually remember the blessings that we have received in Christ.

EXPLORING THE TEXT

The Incarnation of the Word of Life (1 John 1:1–4)

¹ That which was from the beginning, which we have heard, which we have seen with our eyes, which we have looked upon, and our hands have handled, concerning the Word of life—² the life was manifested, and we have seen, and bear witness, and declare to you that eternal life which was with the Father and was manifested to us—³ that which we have seen and heard we declare to you, that you also may have fellowship with us; and truly our fellowship is with the Father and with His Son Jesus Christ. ⁴ And these things we write to you that your joy may be full.

1. John opens this letter in a similar way as he opens his Gospel— by stating that Jesus has existed "from the beginning." However, here John goes on to stress Jesus' humanity, reminding his readers that he was an eyewitness to the early ministry of the "Word of life." Some of the false teachers in the church were claiming that Jesus did not come in a physical body. How does John immediately counter this argument (see verses 1–2)?

_____

_____

_____

_____

_____

_____

2. John states that he has declared these truths to his readers so they may "have fellowship with" him and his fellow apostles. He is thus drawing a distinction between two groups: (1) those who follow the gospel he has preached, and (2) those who follow the false teachers. What does he say are the benefits of belonging to the first group (see verses 3–4)?

_____

_____

_____

_____

_____

_____

_____

_____

_____

Fellowship with Christ and One Another (1 John 1:5–10)

5 This is the message which we have heard from Him and declare to you, that God is light and in Him is no darkness at all. 6 If we say that we have fellowship with Him, and walk in darkness, we lie and do not practice the truth. 7 But if we walk in the light as He is in the light, we have fellowship with one another, and the blood of Jesus Christ His Son cleanses us from all sin.

8 If we say that we have no sin, we deceive ourselves, and the truth is not in us. 9 If we confess our sins, He is faithful and just to forgive us our sins and to cleanse us from all unrighteousness. 10 If we say that we have not sinned, we make Him a liar, and His word is not in us.

3. John now reminds his readers of a foundational truth of the gospel: "God is light and in Him is no darkness." The implication is that those who have fellowship with God will also have no darkness within them. They will instead "walk in the light," which refers to not just an occasional stroll but a routine and a way of life. What are the benefits that believers can receive from this continual practice of walking in the light (see verse 7)?

_____

_____

_____

_____

_____

_____

_____

4. John provides another "test" to distinguish between a follower of Christ and a follower of the world: those who are in Christ confess their sins, which means to agree with God that they are indeed sinners in need of His mercy. How does God respond to this humble realization and confession (see verses 8–9)?

_____

_____

_____

_____

_____

_____

_____

GOING DEEPER

John opens this letter with a reminder to his readers that they have experienced God's grace through Jesus, "the Word of Life" (verse 1). He desires for them to consider what this means—to truly comprehend the gift of salvation they have received so their "joy may be full" (verse 4). John is here reinforcing an idea that Jesus first presented during his ministry on earth, when he told His disciples that He had come to bring abundant life.

5

Jesus the Good Shepherd (John 10:7–11)

> ⁷ Then Jesus said to them again, "Most assuredly, I say to you, I am the door of the sheep. ⁸ All who ever came before Me are thieves and robbers, but the sheep did not hear them. ⁹ I am the door. If anyone enters by Me, he will be saved, and will go in and out and find pasture. ¹⁰ The thief does not come except to steal, and to kill, and to destroy. I have come that they may have life, and that they may have it more abundantly. ¹¹ I am the good shepherd. The good shepherd gives His life for the sheep."

5. In Jesus' day, shepherds would often lay down across the entry of the sheepfold, acting as a "door" to keep wild beasts out and to keep the sheep in. What happens when we access the door that Jesus, the Good Shepherd, embodies for us (see verses 7–9)?

_____

_____

_____

_____

_____

6. The word *life* in this context refers not just to the endlessness of eternal life that we will enjoy in the future but also to a quality of life that we can have right now on earth. How does John describe the type of life we can have today? (see verses 10–11)?

_____

_____

_____

_____

_____

In the book of Acts, many people accepted Jesus' offer to step through the "door" and experience the abundant life He had promised. These individuals realized they were members of a new fellowship that was different from any other group they had belonged to in the past. They recognized the gift they had received and joyfully loved and served one another.

A New Way of Life in Christ (Acts 4:32–37)

32 Now the multitude of those who believed were of one heart and one soul; neither did anyone say that any of the things he possessed was his own, but they had all things in common. 33 And with great power the apostles gave witness to the resurrection of the Lord Jesus. And great grace was upon them all. 34 Nor was there anyone among them who lacked; for all who were possessors of lands or houses sold them, and brought the proceeds of the things that were sold, 35 and laid them at the apostles' feet; and they distributed to each as anyone had need.

7. How does Luke, the author of Acts, describe the attitude of the early Christians? What did they do to bring others into the church (see verses 32–33)?

8. In the early church, just as in churches today, there were some members who had great wealth, land, and possessions, and some who lacked resources and had great need. How did the wealthier believers show love for those in need in the church (see verses 34–35)?

_____

_____

_____

_____

_____

_____

_____

REVIEWING THE STORY

The apostle John was an expert on joy. He had been given the unique privilege of spending three-and-a-half years in Jesus' presence, during which time he witnessed his Lord teaching, performing miracles, and serving others out of love. John had also been present when Jesus died on the cross and three days later rose from the dead. In this opening section of his letter, he reminds his readers of these truths and encourages them to be joyful in their fellowship with one another. He also sets out several "tests" for knowing those who are walking in the light—living in obedience to God—and those who are walking in the darkness of the world.

9. What joy-inspiring things did John convey to his readers (see 1 John 1:1–3)?

_____

_____

_____

_____

_____

_____

_____

10. With whom do believers get to enjoy fellowship (see 1 John 1:3)?

11. What happens when we walk in the light (see 1 John 1:7)?

12. What promise can we cling to when we stumble into sin (see 1 John 1:9)?

APPLYING THE MESSAGE

13. How would you describe the joy you experienced when you first met Christ? What do you most remember about that time when you first encountered the gospel?

_____

_____

_____

_____

_____

_____

_____

14. What does it look like in your life to "walk in the light"? What practices have you developed to help you abide in God's light?

_____

_____

_____

_____

_____

_____

REFLECTING ON THE MEANING

John opens his first letter by encouraging us to consider the incredible gift of salvation that we been given in Christ. This realization should lead to great joy in our lives—however, as we all know only too well, not every Christian experiences such joy. Perhaps this is why John also warns us about three things that can cause us to forfeit the joy that is ours in Christ.

First, we forfeit our joy when we deny the power of sin. Note John's argument in verse 5: "God is light and in Him is no darkness at all." If there is darkness in us, we cannot have fellowship with God. If we cannot have fellowship with Him, we can have no joy. Therefore, we forfeit our joy by walking in darkness. What is the cure? It is found in verse 7. At the moment we realize we are drifting into darkness we have to turn around and go back toward the light. We go back to church, back to the Word, back to our Christian friends who walk in the light. This is a choice of the will, not of the feelings. Some things in life we have to do because they are right or the best or wise. And walking back toward the light is one of those things.

Second, we forfeit our joy when we deny the presence of sin. John writes, "If we say that we have no sin, we deceive ourselves" (verse 8). Some people claim that when we give our lives to Christ, our sin nature is eradicated and we are left only with a perfect new nature. But that is not true. In reality, our old nature just contends with our new nature. The cure for our sinfulness is not to deny it exists but to rely on God to forgive us. Our responsibility is to agree with God and admit we *do* have sin within us. When that happens, we are in one accord with God and the blood of Christ cleanses us from our sin. We maintain the joy of our salvation.

Third, we forfeit our joy when we deny the practice of sin. John writes, "If we say that we have not sinned, we make Him a liar, and His word is not in us" (verse 10). Unlike the situation where we deny the *presence* of sin—that we have the ability to sin—to deny the *practice* of sin means to deny that we have sinned in a given instance. In other words, we rationalize or justify of our sin and refuse to admit that what we did was sin before God. Once again, the solution is Christ the Righteous One. He stands before God as our attorney, defending us against the claims of Satan the accuser. Christ's righteousness is the solution to our unrighteousness.

If you lose your joy in the Christian life, examine John's three examples. The chances are good that you will find in such an examination the cause for the short-circuiting of your joy. In the process, you will also find the cure—and your joy will be restored.

JOURNALING YOUR RESPONSE

Which of these joy-killers do you struggle with the most in your relationship with Christ? What steps have you taken to defeat these joy-killers so you can experience God's abundant life?

TRUST AND OBEY

1 John 2:1–14

GETTING STARTED

In what areas of life do you find it most difficult to obey God?

_____

_____

_____

_____

_____

_____

_____

_____

_____

_____

_____

_____

SETTING THE STAGE

When eighty-one-year-old Robert Kupferschmid went flying with his friend one day in a single-engine plane, he had no idea that he was about to become the *pilot*. During the journey, his friend, who was flying the small plane, suddenly slumped over the controls and died. Robert grabbed the flight stick, got on the radio, and cried out for help.

Two pilots flying nearby heard the distress call and started feeding Robert instructions about how to fly the aircraft and land it. They guided him to the nearest airport and had him circle the field three times until he felt ready to set the plane down on the runway. The plane made a bouncing landing and finally came to rest in the grass next to the runway. The first-time pilot suffered no injuries.

Now, just imagine what would have happened if Robert Kupferschmid, a totally inexperienced pilot, had debated with the pilots trying to coach him to the ground. Can you imagine him saying, "I need to pray about that last directive you gave me"? No, he knew that his life depended on obeying the instructions of those who had the wisdom he desperately needed. So he obeyed every word he was given . . . and it saved his life.

The apostle John has much to say about this kind of obedience. In this next section of his letter, he talks about the central role that following God's instructions plays in our faith. Sadly, many of us today overestimate our own powers of discernment and decision-making. We refuse to heed the guidance of the One who has *much* greater experience than we have and can guide us safely to the ground. As John makes it clear in this chapter, such an assumption is a fatal mistake, for our spiritual survival *depends* on our willingness to obey the directives that come from God.

EXPLORING THE TEXT

The Test of Knowing Christ (1 John 2:1–8)

---

¹ My little children, these things I write to you, so that you may not sin. And if anyone sins, we have an Advocate with the Father, Jesus Christ the righteous. ² And He Himself is the propitiation for our sins, and not for ours only but also for the whole world.

³ Now by this we know that we know Him, if we keep His commandments. ⁴ He who says, "I know Him," and does not keep His

commandments, is a liar, and the truth is not in him. [5] But whoever keeps His word, truly the love of God is perfected in him. By this we know that we are in Him. [6] He who says he abides in Him ought himself also to walk just as He walked.

[7] Brethren, I write no new commandment to you, but an old commandment which you have had from the beginning. The old commandment is the word which you heard from the beginning. [8] Again, a new commandment I write to you, which thing is true in Him and in you, because the darkness is passing away, and the true light is already shining.

---

1. John is careful to note that just because God *forgives* sin does not give a person the *license* to sin. Rather, he is writing these words so that we "may not sin." However, what promise are we given if we do sin? For whom is this provision available (see verses 1–2)?

_____

_____

_____

_____

_____

_____

_____

_____

_____

_____

_____

2. John has established the doctrinal differences between those who "walk in the light" and those who "walk in darkness" in the first chapter of his letter. He now addresses the behavioral differences that exists between the two groups. What does John say is the "test" that determines if a person truly knows God (see verses 3–7)?

_____

_____

_____

_____

_____

_____

_____

The Test of Walking with Christ (1 John 2:9–14)

⁹ He who says he is in the light, and hates his brother, is in darkness until now. ¹⁰ He who loves his brother abides in the light, and there is no cause for stumbling in him. ¹¹ But he who hates his brother is in darkness and walks in darkness, and does not know where he is going, because the darkness has blinded his eyes.

¹² I write to you, little children,
Because your sins are forgiven you for His name's sake.
¹³ I write to you, fathers,
Because you have known Him who is from the beginning.
I write to you, young men,
Because you have overcome the wicked one.
I write to you, little children,
Because you have known the Father.
¹⁴ I have written to you, fathers,
Because you have known Him who is from the beginning.
I have written to you, young men,
Because you are strong, and the word of God abides in you,
And you have overcome the wicked one.

3. John has now clarified that a person who *knows* God is a person who *obeys* God. He now provides a key test for determining whether that person is truly walking in the path that Jesus set for all His followers. What is this test (see verses 9–11)?

_____

_____

_____

_____

_____

_____

_____

4. John closes with a series of slogans that were likely familiar to his audience. Notice that he classifies his readers into three spiritual groups: little children, fathers, and young men. What reason does he give for writing to each group (see verses 12–14)?

_____

_____

_____

_____

_____

_____

_____

GOING DEEPER

John was not the only person in the Bible to stress the difference between those who merely *say* they follow Christ and those who actually *prove* they follow Christ by obeying His commands. In John's Gospel, he records what Jesus Himself said about those who truly follow Him. James would later emphasize the same point in his letter to the churches.

The Indwelling of the Father and Son (John 14:19–24)

19 "A little while longer and the world will see Me no more, but you will see Me. Because I live, you will live also. 20 At that day you will know that I am in My Father, and you in Me, and I in you. 21 He who has My commandments and keeps them, it is he who loves Me. And he who loves Me will be loved by My Father, and I will love him and manifest Myself to him."

22 Judas (not Iscariot) said to Him, "Lord, how is it that You will manifest Yourself to us, and not to the world?"

23 Jesus answered and said to him, "If anyone loves Me, he will keep My word; and My Father will love him, and We will come to him and make Our home with him. 24 He who does not love Me does not keep My words; and the word which you hear is not Mine but the Father's who sent Me.

5. Jesus spoke these words to prepare His disciples for His death and resurrection. In a little while He would no longer be with them on the earth, but they could be comforted in knowing He would always dwell within them. What does Jesus say that those who desire this indwelling with do? Who is the one who "loves" Christ (see verses 19–21)?

6. Jesus' words must have come as a surprise to the disciples, who were expecting the Messiah to be a political figure who would deliver Israel from the Roman Empire. What did Jesus, the Messiah, promise to do instead for those who obey God (see verses 22–24)?

_____

_____

_____

_____

_____

Doers of the Word (James 1:23–27)

23 For if anyone is a hearer of the word and not a doer, he is like a man observing his natural face in a mirror; 24 for he observes himself, goes away, and immediately forgets what kind of man he was. 25 But he who looks into the perfect law of liberty and continues in it, and is not a forgetful hearer but a doer of the work, this one will be blessed in what he does.

26 If anyone among you thinks he is religious, and does not bridle his tongue but deceives his own heart, this one's religion is useless. 27 Pure and undefiled religion before God and the Father is this: to visit orphans and widows in their trouble, and to keep oneself unspotted from the world.

7. James uses the analogy of a man looking into a mirror and then immediately forgetting what he looks like to illustrate the fallacy of those who say they follow Christ but do not obey His commands. What is the "proof" of a true follower of Jesus (see verses 23–25)?

_____

_____

_____

_____

8. James states that those who are "doers" of God's Word will investigate what the Bible says and allow its teachings to influence their actions. What are some of the signs that such a transformation is taking place (see verses 25–27)?

_____

_____

_____

_____

_____

_____

REVIEWING THE STORY

The apostle John identifies the litmus test for discipleship: _obedience_. Often actions speak louder than words in the Christian faith, and those who genuinely know Jesus will obey His commands to love God and love others. John reminds his readers that this is not a new instruction he is giving to them—it is one they were given from the beginning. But it is a vital command, for it distinguishes those who walk in the light and those who walk in darkness. John closes with a series of exhortations for "children," "fathers," and "young men" in the faith.

9. What does John say about someone who claims to know Christ but does not keep His commandments (see 1 John 2:4)?

_____

_____

_____

_____

_____

_____

10. What happens when we keep God's Word (see 1 John 2:5)?

_____

_____

_____

_____

_____

_____

_____

11. What happens when we "hate" our Christian brothers and sisters— or reject fellowship with them (see 1 John 2:9–11)?

_____

_____

_____

_____

_____

_____

12. What happens when the Word of God truly abides within us (see 1 John 2:14)?

_____

_____

_____

_____

_____

_____

_____

APPLYING THE MESSAGE

13. How are you demonstrating that you are a follower of Christ in both word *and* deed?

_____

_____

_____

_____

_____

_____

_____

_____

14. What are some ways that you can love your fellow brothers and sisters in Christ?

_____

_____

_____

_____

_____

_____

_____

_____

REFLECTING ON THE MEANING

Just as children enjoy a happier relationship with their parents when they obey them, so we enjoy a happier relationship with our heavenly Father when we obey Him. Most of us spend our entire lives trying to learn the simplicity of this truth. We try every way imaginable to have a joyful relationship with God without doing the one thing that is the key: obey His commands! In 1 John 2:6–8, the apostle emphasizes three key points about this kind of obedience.

First, the example of obedience. The example John gives us to follow—a person who actually loved the way John is encouraging us to love—is Jesus Himself. "He who says he abides in Him ought himself also to walk just as He walked" (verse 6). Jesus' secret was to walk in total dependence on His Father. He didn't set His own agenda, develop His own plans, or think up His own ideas. Only by the power of the Holy Spirit—the same Spirit who filled Jesus without measure (see John 3:34)—can we hope to walk as Jesus walked.

Second, the expectation of obedience. John states that what he is telling us is nothing new (see 2:6). The command to love God and one another goes all the way back to the Old Testament (see Leviticus 19:18 and Deuteronomy 6:5). Jesus even stressed that love for God and one's neighbor are the *greatest* commands (see Matthew 22:37–39). Those two laws are the foundation of everything else. Our relationship with God is based on loving Him and loving others—and we do this when we keep His commands.

Third, the explanation of obedience. John says in verse 7 that he is not giving a new commandment, but then in verse 8, he makes reference to a new commandment. The "newness" has to do with the standard to which Jesus raised the old commandment. Perhaps William Barclay, the Scottish theologian and Bible commentator, gave the best explanation: "The commandment to love was old in the sense that men had known it for a long time; but the commandment to love was new, because in Jesus Christ love reached a standard which it never reached before, and it was by that standard that men were commanded to love."

If you want to walk in love like Jesus walked, you must learn to walk in obedience to God as Jesus did. A great prayer to pray before you enter into any situation in which your obedience may be tested is, "Lord, help me to bring Jesus into this situation." When people see the love and peace of God in your life, they will be drawn to Jesus. They will know that you love God and are living in fellowship with Him.

JOURNALING YOUR RESPONSE

How does your life demonstrate to others that you are living in fellowship with God?

LOVING THE WORLD

1 John 2:15–29

GETTING STARTED

What immediately comes to mind when you picture "the world"?

_____

_____

_____

_____

_____

_____

_____

_____

_____

_____

_____

_____

_____

_____

_____

_____

SETTING THE STAGE

As we arrive at this next section of John's letter, we read this interesting imperative: "Do not love the world or the things in the world" (1 John 2:15). At first reading, it can be difficult to know what John is instructing us to do. After all, we are residents of the world, so it is only natural that we are going to love some of the things in it. Furthermore, didn't God Himself tell us that He "so loved the world that He gave His only begotten Son" (John 3:16)?

The key to understanding John's instruction is to know what is meant by "the world." John clarifies that he is referring to a system being orchestrated by the devil—"The lust of the flesh, the lust of the eyes, and the pride of life" (1 John 2:16). The system of the world in which we live is not a passive or neutral place. Rather, it is energized by the "ruler of this world" (John 12:31) with a mission: *to confront and defeat the kingdom of God*. Satan, our great enemy, is out to defeat us at every turn and derail our walk with God.

John understood this reality. In this section of his letter, he provides some foundational teachings about the things of this world and how we can grow in spiritual maturity in spite of the fact that we live in a world that is against us. John's critical point is this: *the Christian life cannot be lived from the outside in*. It must be lived from the inside out. We *will* be influenced by the world, so we have to be grounded in our relationship with Christ. What we participate in or abstain from must have the glory of God as its foundation. We do what we do because we love the Lord, not because we want to conform to someone's code of behavior.

EXPLORING THE TEXT

Do Not Love the World (1 John 2:15–23)

15 Do not love the world or the things in the world. If anyone loves the world, the love of the Father is not in him. 16 For all that is in

the world—the lust of the flesh, the lust of the eyes, and the pride of life—is not of the Father but is of the world. ¹⁷ And the world is passing away, and the lust of it; but he who does the will of God abides forever.

¹⁸ Little children, it is the last hour; and as you have heard that the Antichrist is coming, even now many antichrists have come, by which we know that it is the last hour. ¹⁹ They went out from us, but they were not of us; for if they had been of us, they would have continued with us; but they went out that they might be made manifest, that none of them were of us.

²⁰ But you have an anointing from the Holy One, and you know all things. ²¹ I have not written to you because you do not know the truth, but because you know it, and that no lie is of the truth.

²² Who is a liar but he who denies that Jesus is the Christ? He is antichrist who denies the Father and the Son. ²³ Whoever denies the Son does not have the Father either; he who acknowledges the Son has the Father also.

---

1. John opens with an instruction for his readers to not "love the world." However, in making this statement, he is *not* advising them to cease interactions with non-believers or abstain from participating in life on this planet. Rather, what three things does he not want them to "love"? What is the consequence of loving these things (see verses 15–17)?

2. John stresses that his readers are living in the "last hour" and that "many antichrists have come." In other words, Jesus could return at any moment, so they needed to stand firm in the truth of the gospel and reject fine-sounding arguments by the "antichrists" (which literally means "those against Christ). What does John say about these individuals? What do true believers in Christ have (see verses 18–23)?

_____

_____

_____

_____

_____

_____

_____

Let Truth Abide in You (1 John 2:24–29)

24 Therefore let that abide in you which you heard from the beginning. If what you heard from the beginning abides in you, you also will abide in the Son and in the Father. 25 And this is the promise that He has promised us—eternal life.

26 These things I have written to you concerning those who try to deceive you. 27 But the anointing which you have received from Him abides in you, and you do not need that anyone teach you; but as the same anointing teaches you concerning all things, and is true, and is not a lie, and just as it has taught you, you will abide in Him.

28 And now, little children, abide in Him, that when He appears, we may have confidence and not be ashamed before Him at His coming. 29 If you know that He is righteous, you know that everyone who practices righteousness is born of Him.

3. John reminds his readers of the message they had "heard from the beginning," which refers to the gospel they had received from himself and the other apostles. What is the promise for those who abide in this truth? Why is John reminding them of it (see verses 24–27)?

_____

_____

_____

_____

4. John closes with another reminder to his readers that Jesus could return at any time. Why does he want them to abide in Christ in light of this fact (see verses 28–29)?

_____

_____

_____

_____

GOING DEEPER

John reveals two groups of people in this section of his letter: (1) those who acknowledge Jesus as the Son of God and abide in His ways, and (2) those who chase after the things of this world and prove by their actions that they are not abiding in God. Jesus also made this distinction during His ministry on earth. In the following passage, we read how He challenged the Jewish religious leaders on this point and called them to consider who they were _truly_ following.

Abraham's Seed and Satan Seed (John 8:37–47)

> [37] [Jesus said], "I know that you are Abraham's descendants, but you seek to kill Me, because My word has no place in you. [38] I speak what I have seen with My Father, and you do what you have seen with your father."

³⁹ They answered and said to Him, "Abraham is our father."

Jesus said to them, "If you were Abraham's children, you would do the works of Abraham. ⁴⁰ But now you seek to kill Me, a Man who has told you the truth which I heard from God. Abraham did not do this. ⁴¹ You do the deeds of your father."

Then they said to Him, "We were not born of fornication; we have one Father—God."

⁴² Jesus said to them, "If God were your Father, you would love Me, for I proceeded forth and came from God; nor have I come of Myself, but He sent Me. ⁴³ Why do you not understand My speech? Because you are not able to listen to My word. ⁴⁴ You are of your father the devil, and the desires of your father you want to do. He was a murderer from the beginning, and does not stand in the truth, because there is no truth in him. When he speaks a lie, he speaks from his own resources, for he is a liar and the father of it. ⁴⁵ But because I tell the truth, you do not believe Me. ⁴⁶ Which of you convicts Me of sin? And if I tell the truth, why do you not believe Me? ⁴⁷ He who is of God hears God's words; therefore you do not hear, because you are not of God.

---

7. The Pharisees believed they were guaranteed a place in heaven because they were descendants of Abraham. How does Jesus respond to their claim (see verses 39–41)?

_____

_____

_____

_____

_____

_____

_____

8. Jesus used the phrase *your father* to identify the source of the Pharisees' worldly actions. How did the devil exercise control over the Pharisees (see verses 41–47)?

_____

_____

_____

_____

_____

_____

_____

The apostle Paul also recognized the need for believers to separate themselves from the things of this world. In the book of Colossians, he urges a group of believers to set their hearts and minds on pursuing God above all else. As Paul notes, they are to actually "put to death" the sinful practices of their former lives so that they can wholeheartedly follow after Christ.

Not Carnality but Christ (Colossians 3:1–14)

¹ If then you were raised with Christ, seek those things which are above, where Christ is, sitting at the right hand of God. ² Set your mind on things above, not on things on the earth. ³ For you died, and your life is hidden with Christ in God. ⁴ When Christ who is our life appears, then you also will appear with Him in glory.

⁵ Therefore put to death your members which are on the earth: fornication, uncleanness, passion, evil desire, and covetousness, which is idolatry. ⁶ Because of these things the wrath of God is coming upon the sons of disobedience, ⁷ in which you yourselves once walked when you lived in them.

⁸ But now you yourselves are to put off all these: anger, wrath, malice, blasphemy, filthy language out of your mouth. ⁹ Do not lie to one another, since you have put off the old man with his deeds, ¹⁰ and have put on the new man who is renewed in knowledge according to

the image of Him who created him, ¹¹ where there is neither Greek nor Jew, circumcised nor uncircumcised, barbarian, Scythian, slave nor free, but Christ is all and in all.

¹² Therefore, as the elect of God, holy and beloved, put on tender mercies, kindness, humility, meekness, longsuffering; ¹³ bearing with one another, and forgiving one another, if anyone has a complaint against another; even as Christ forgave you, so you also must do. ¹⁴ But above all these things put on love, which is the bond of perfection.

---

5. Paul doesn't mince words in describing how believers should respond to the things of this world. What does he urge us to put to death and rid ourselves of (see verses 1–8)?

_____

_____

_____

_____

_____

_____

6. Paul states that loving the things of God involves more than just an inward focus. How do we reflect God's priorities in the way that we treat others (see verses 9–14)?

_____

_____

_____

_____

_____

_____

_____

REVIEWING THE STORY

John identifies the stark choice that believers face: we can either love the world and desire the things in it, or we can love God and desire to follow His will. If we choose to love the world, the love of God is not within us—and we will miss out on God's blessings. This warning is especially critical because we are living in the "last days" when Jesus could return to the earth at any time. We must reject any teaching that is against Christ as we allow God's truth to abide within us. As we do this, we will be able to see through the enemy's deceptions.

9. What categories does John use to encompass all that is in the world (see 1 John 2:15–17)?

_____

_____

_____

_____

10. How does John say that we can know this is the "last hour" (see 1 John 2:18–19)?

_____

_____

_____

_____

11. What promise sets the things of God above the things of the world (see 1 John 2:24–26)?

_____

_____

_____

_____

12. What does John say about those who practice righteousness (see 1 John 2:28–29)?

_____

_____

_____

_____

_____

APPLYING THE MESSAGE

13. How do you keep your focus on loving Jesus rather than the things of this world?

_____

_____

_____

_____

_____

14. How can you best help other believers keep this same focus in their lives?

_____

_____

_____

_____

_____

REFLECTING ON THE MEANING

There are three different ways that the term _world_ is used in the New Testament. The first refers to our planet earth (see Acts 17:24), and we can certainly love and revel in its beauty. The second refers to the world of fallen humanity (see John 3:16–17), and we certainly are called to love the "world" in this sense as God so loved it. The third refers to the corrupt world system we see operating each day, with all its intrigues, undercurrents, temptations, and schemes at work. This is the "world" that John instructs us *not* to love (see 1 John 3:15).

But how can this be done? How do we resist the pull of the world when we are living in it and constantly being influenced by it? How can we overcome the world when we find ourselves becoming too friendly with it? John responds to these questions by calling out three "counter-influences" in his letter that can help us break off our friendship with the world.

The first of these influences is *the positive assurance of our faith*. "For whatever is born of God overcomes the world. And this is the victory that has overcome the world—our faith (1 John 5:4). Satan wants us to doubt our salvation. So we need to be sure that we are saved, and then never waver in that faith. Our faith can overcome the temptations of the world.

The second influence is *the presence of the Holy Spirit in our lives*. "You are of God, little children, and have overcome them, because He who is in you is greater than he who is in the world" (1 John 4:4). The reality is that we are no match for Satan. Only in the power of the indwelling Christ, made real in us by the presence of the Holy Spirit, can we hope to withstand the allure of the world. By the power of the Holy Spirit, we *can* overcome the world.

The third influence is *the power of the Word of God in our hearts*. "I have written to you, young men, because you are strong, and the word of God abides in you, and you have overcome the wicked one" (1 John 2:14). By allowing the word of Christ to dwell in us richly, our minds will be renewed on a daily basis, and we will gain strength to resist the enemy.

We all need to consider whether we are overcoming the world in these ways—or whether it is more the case that the world is overcoming us. We cannot toy with this world system. We need to take its threat seriously and look to a source of strength that is greater than ourselves. As we do this, we will find that we can be overcomers in Christ.

JOURNALING YOUR RESPONSE

What specific distractions do you need to put aside to focus more on the things of God?

WE SHALL BE LIKE HIM!

1 John 3:1–12

GETTING STARTED

What are some specific areas in your life where you would like to be more like Christ?

_____

_____

_____

_____

_____

_____

_____

_____

_____

_____

_____

_____

_____

SETTING THE STAGE

John opens this next section of his letter with a declaration: "Behold what manner of love the Father has bestowed on us, that we should be called children of God" (1 John 3:1). The Greek word for *love* that John

37

employs in this verse is *agape*—a kind of love relatively unknown before the New Testament era. *Agape* represents the love that comes from God. It is perfect love that is motivated by pure intentions and seeks only good for the object of its affection.

Agape love is a difficult concept for us to wrap our minds around. The love we give and receive is almost always conditional. *If you do this . . . I will love you. If you fail to do this . . . then I will withhold my love from you.* Sometimes our love gets hijacked by impure motives such as lust, control, or jealousy. Even when our motives are above question, our wisdom and judgment are not. We may think we know what is best for our loved ones, but that is not always the case. As a result, we may hurt the people we love most.

But God's love is different. It expects nothing in return. It is given simply because the Giver wants to give it. It is a love that God extends to *all* of humanity—and with it the invitation to become a part of His own family! Those who accept His offer become "children of God," and they begin a lifelong process of gradually being transformed into the image of God's Son.

Yes, God's love has the power to change us from within and make us more like our Savior! These changes make it possible to recognize His love in our lives and in the lives of others. Because of God's love, we are no longer slaves to sin and unrighteousness. Instead, we can practice the righteousness for which we were created and fulfill our God-given potential.

EXPLORING THE TEXT

The Command to Love (1 John 3:1–6)

> [1] Behold what manner of love the Father has bestowed on us, that we should be called children of God! Therefore the world does not know us, because it did not know Him. [2] Beloved, now we are children of God; and it has not yet been revealed what we shall be, but we know that when He is revealed, we shall be like Him, for we shall see Him as He is. [3] And everyone who has this hope in Him purifies himself, just as He is pure.

⁴ Whoever commits sin also commits lawlessness, and sin is lawlessness. ⁵ And you know that He was manifested to take away our sins, and in Him there is no sin. ⁶ Whoever abides in Him does not sin. Whoever sins has neither seen Him nor known Him.

---

1. John opens this section of his letter by stating that those who have accepted Christ as their Savior now belong to God's family. The result of this transformation is that the world no longer "knows" us—just as the world did not "know" Christ (see John 1:10). What does John say will ultimately be revealed to all members of God's family (see 1 John 3:1–2)?

_____

_____

_____

_____

2. As God's adopted children, we receive all of the benefits of being a part of His family—but we also have responsibilities as members of His family. What are those who have "this hope in Him" and "abide in Him" commanded to do (see verses 3, 6)?

_____

_____

_____

The Imperative of Love (1 John 3:7–12)

⁷ Little children, let no one deceive you. He who practices righteousness is righteous, just as He is righteous. ⁸ He who sins is of the devil, for the devil has sinned from the beginning. For this purpose the Son of God was manifested, that He might destroy the works of the devil. ⁹ Whoever has been born of God does not sin, for His seed remains in him; and he cannot sin, because he has been born of God.

¹⁰ In this the children of God and the children of the devil are manifest: Whoever does not practice righteousness is not of God, nor is he who does not love his brother. ¹¹ For this is the message that you heard from the beginning, that we should love one another, ¹² not as Cain who was of the wicked one and murdered his brother. And why did he murder him? Because his works were evil and his brother's righteous.

---

3. John's warning to "let no one deceive you" indicates that false teachers in the church were threatening to lead the believers astray. What two further "tests" does John put forth to help the believers know if a person has truly been born of God (see verses 7–9)?

_____

_____

_____

4. As members of God's family, we are to follow Christ in righteousness *and* love others as God loved us. What does the Old Testament story of Cain and Abel reveal about what happens when family members do *not* show love to one another (see verses 10–12)?

_____

_____

_____

_____

GOING DEEPER

The apostle John wrote, "When [Jesus] is revealed, we shall be like Him, for we shall see Him as He is" (1 John 3:2). John is referring here specifically to the change that will occur to believers when Jesus returns to this earth—though he is clear that this transformation into Christlikeness begins in this life. The apostle Paul frequently wrote about this same kind of transformation in the last days, as the following passages relate.

The Comfort of Christ's Coming (1 Thessalonians 4:13–18)

 13 But I do not want you to be ignorant, brethren, concerning those who have fallen asleep, lest you sorrow as others who have no hope. 14 For if we believe that Jesus died and rose again, even so God will bring with Him those who sleep in Jesus.

15 For this we say to you by the word of the Lord, that we who are alive and remain until the coming of the Lord will by no means precede those who are asleep. 16 For the Lord Himself will descend from heaven with a shout, with the voice of an archangel, and with the trumpet of God. And the dead in Christ will rise first. 17 Then we who are alive and remain shall be caught up together with them in the clouds to meet the Lord in the air. And thus we shall always be with the Lord. 18 Therefore comfort one another with these words.

5. Paul's mention of "those who have fallen asleep" refers to members of the Thessalonian church who had died. Possibly, these were new converts in the church, and there was great concern about what would happen to them. What hope does Paul give to the believers to comfort them and allay their concerns (see verses 13–14)?

_____

_____

_____

_____

_____

6. While the details of the Rapture that Paul describes are intriguing, the most important takeaway is that we will always be with the Lord.

As we keep this reality in mind, what should God's love motivate us to do for others (see verses 15–18)?

_____

_____

_____

_____

_____

Our Citizenship in Heaven (Philippians 3:17–21)

¹⁷ Brethren, join in following my example, and note those who so walk, as you have us for a pattern. ¹⁸ For many walk, of whom I have told you often, and now tell you even weeping, that they are the enemies of the cross of Christ: ¹⁹ whose end is destruction, whose god is their belly, and whose glory is in their shame—who set their mind on earthly things. ²⁰ For our citizenship is in heaven, from which we also eagerly wait for the Savior, the Lord Jesus Christ, ²¹ who will transform our lowly body that it may be conformed to His glorious body, according to the working by which He is able even to subdue all things to Himself.

7. Paul encourages the Philippian believers to follow the godly example that he and others have set on how to live for Christ. Why does he issue this instruction (see verses 17–18)?

_____

_____

_____

_____

_____

8. What does Paul say to his readers in regard to their "citizenship"? What can believers expect when Jesus returns (see verses 20–21)?

REVIEWING THE STORY

John explains that God the Father so loved us that He adopted us into His family. He is now transforming us into the image of Christ—a process that will be complete when we see Jesus as He is. The hope of this transformation impacts every area of our lives. It enables us to pursue righteousness and love others. It separates us from the world and from the schemes of the devil. It frees us from the bondage of sin. We cannot live like those who claim to have God's love but refuse His call to righteous living.

9. What privilege does God's love bestow on us (see 1 John 3:1)?

---

10. What is true of someone who has hope in God (see 1 John 3:3)?

---

11. How can we recognize the presence of God's love in someone's life (see 1 John 3:7–9)?

_____

_____

_____

_____

12. Who does John use as an example of what can happen when God's love doesn't penetrate our hearts (see 1 John 3:11–12)?

_____

_____

_____

_____

Applying the Message

13. What are some areas in your life where you need to pursue greater righteousness?

_____

_____

_____

_____

14. What is one practical way that you could show love today to a brother and sister in Christ?

_____

_____

_____

_____

REFLECTING ON THE MEANING

John makes this claim: "Beloved, now we are children of God; and it has not yet been revealed what we shall be, but we know that when He is revealed, we shall be like Him" (1 John 3:2). There are many things that we do not know about this day when Jesus will be revealed. However, there are three things that we can know for sure about this time in the future.

First, *we can know that Jesus will appear.* The Bible is filled with this truth. In fact, there is more revelation in Scripture about Jesus' second coming than His first coming. History is marked by time before Christ and since Christ—and His second appearing will be no less historic, as it will begins the end of time as we know it and usher in the eternal state.

Second, *we can know that we will be like Christ.* In this life, we seek to follow the example of Jesus so that we can become more like Him in our thoughts, attitudes, and actions. But even the godliest saint in this fallen world will never be *completely* like Christ. All that will change on the day that Jesus returns to this earth. We will be changed instantaneously and become just like Christ. It will all happen in "the twinkling of an eye" (1 Corinthians 15:52).

Third, *we can know that we shall see Christ as He truly is.* We are on a journey in this life of drawing closer to Jesus and abiding in Him so that we can witness His glory. But this journey will not be complete until that day when Jesus returns and we become fully like Him. In the meantime, we must be continually moving in the direction of Christlikeness. We all should be able to say, "I'm not yet what I should be or want to be, but neither am I what I used to be."

John's point is that the more time we spend with Jesus, the more we will become like Him until He returns. Is this not good news? God loved us so much that He sent His Son to die for us. But His love will continue in the future, as He causes us to become like His Son. We have the greatest hope of any people on earth! Regardless of what happens to us in this life, we know Christ will appear, we will see Him as He is, and we will become like Him for all eternity.

JOURNALING YOUR RESPONSE

What comes to your mind when you picture the day that you will see Christ and become fully like Him?

THE PROBLEM WITH HATE

1 John 3:13–24

GETTING STARTED

What are some of the results of hate that you have seen in the world?

_____

_____

_____

_____

_____

_____

_____

_____

_____

_____

_____

_____

_____

_____

_____

_____

_____

_____

_____

SETTING THE STAGE

One of the ironies of modern life is that as our world becomes more connected through advances in technology, our society becomes more fractured and divided. We are discovering that social media can be anything but social. In fact, much of it fosters animosity and hatred. The impersonal and immediate nature of the technology seems to invite toxicity. We are encouraged to vent our emotions while they are fresh and are rewarded with "likes" and approving messages when our comments cut deep. We are no longer guided by the social cues that used to govern—and keep civil—most face-to-face interactions.

As a result, many of us today—Christians included—are finding it easy to justify less-than-loving behavior and attitudes. We get caught up in the us-versus-them dynamic of the world. We define ourselves by what we oppose and portray ourselves as "culture warriors," battling influences that we believe are dangerous to our cause. Convinced of our own rightness and morality, we do not hesitate to empty both barrels at anyone who dares to cross us! Unfortunately, the first thing that gets lost in these skirmishes, no matter how noble they may seem, are the three words that Jesus hammered home to His followers: *love your neighbor.*

In the next section of John's letter, the disciple whom Jesus loved shares his unique insights into this three-word commandment from Christ. John portrays love for others as a natural outworking of our Christian faith—so natural, in fact, that if it is absent, our faith can be questioned. We are not called to respond in kind when we experience hatred. We are called to a higher standard. We are called to sacrificial love.

EXPLORING THE TEXT

The Outworking of Love (1 John 3:13–17)

¹³ Do not marvel, my brethren, if the world hates you. ¹⁴ We know that we have passed from death to life, because we love the brethren. He

who does not love his brother abides in death. [15] Whoever hates his brother is a murderer, and you know that no murderer has eternal life abiding in him.

[16] By this we know love, because He laid down His life for us. And we also ought to lay down our lives for the brethren. [17] But whoever has this world's goods, and sees his brother in need, and shuts up his heart from him, how does the love of God abide in him?

---

1. The apostle John expresses no surprise that the world system—which is orchestrated by Satan—would hate true followers of Christ. The reason is because those who have accepted salvation have "passed from death to life" and the world no longer has any claim on them. But what does John say is the "test" of knowing that a person is truly abiding in Christ (see verses 13–15)?

_____

_____

_____

_____

_____

_____

2. John's comment about "this world's goods" refers to material objects that sustain life, such as food, clothing, and shelter. How can sharing these goods be an expression of God's love? What does it say about us if we *do not* help those in need (see verses 16–17)?

_____

_____

_____

_____

_____

_____

_____

The Spirit of Truth and the Spirit of Error (1 John 3:18–24)

¹⁸ My little children, let us not love in word or in tongue, but in deed and in truth. ¹⁹ And by this we know that we are of the truth, and shall assure our hearts before Him. ²⁰ For if our heart condemns us, God is greater than our heart, and knows all things. ²¹ Beloved, if our heart does not condemn us, we have confidence toward God. ²² And whatever we ask we receive from Him, because we keep His commandments and do those things that are pleasing in His sight. ²³ And this is His commandment: that we should believe on the name of His Son Jesus Christ and love one another, as He gave us commandment.

²⁴ Now he who keeps His commandments abides in Him, and He in him. And by this we know that He abides in us, by the Spirit whom He has given us.

3. John's use of the phrase "my little children" indicates that he is now addressing true believers in Christ. He encourages these followers to "not love in word or tongue" only, which means to speak loving words but stop short of acting on those words. What are some of the benefits that believers can expect to experience when they love in word *and* deeds (see verses 18–23)?

_____

_____

_____

_____

_____

_____

_____

_____

_____

4. The indwelling to which John refers to is mutual—Jesus in us and us in Him. What is the evidence of our dwelling in Christ and His dwelling in us (see verse 24)?

_____

_____

_____

_____

_____

_____

_____

_____

_____

GOING DEEPER

As previously discussed, the command for God's people to love one another is nothing new. The Bible is filled with countless exhortations to love one another and to demonstrate that love through both words and actions. In the book of Proverbs, we find King Solomon, one of the wisest men who ever lived, sharing his wisdom on this topic, one valuable nugget at a time. In the following passage, he offers stark warnings about giving hate a platform in our lives.

Wisdom and Love (Proverbs 10:12–18)

¹² Hatred stirs up strife, but love covers all sins.

¹³ Wisdom is found on the lips of him who has understanding, but a rod is for the back of him who is devoid of understanding.

¹⁴ Wise people store up knowledge, but the mouth of the foolish is near destruction.

¹⁵ The rich man's wealth is his strong city; the destruction of the poor is their poverty.

16 The labor of the righteous leads to life, the wages of the wicked to sin.

17 He who keeps instruction is in the way of life, but he who refuses correction goes astray.

18 Whoever hides hatred has lying lips, and whoever spreads slander is a fool.

---

5. Solomon notes that love doesn't just hide our sins but actually reconciles us to one another. What happens when hatred is given a voice (see verse 12)?

_____

_____

_____

_____

_____

_____

6. What characteristics distinguish a wise person from a foolish person? Why is it important for us to be loving not only in actions but also with our words (see verses 13–18)?

_____

_____

_____

_____

_____

_____

Jesus also had much to say on the need for followers of God to show love to one another—and the consequences that result when we fail to follow this command. In the following passage, Jesus states that anyone who is even *angry* with his brother will be subject to judgment. The basic principle, also emphasized by John, is that hate and murder are cut from the same cloth.

Murder Begins in the Heart (Matthew 5:21–26)

21 "You have heard that it was said to those of old, 'You shall not murder, and whoever murders will be in danger of the judgment.' 22 But I say to you that whoever is angry with his brother without a cause shall be in danger of the judgment. And whoever says to his brother, 'Raca!' shall be in danger of the council. But whoever says, 'You fool!' shall be in danger of hell fire. 23 Therefore if you bring your gift to the altar, and there remember that your brother has something against you, 24 leave your gift there before the altar, and go your way. First be reconciled to your brother, and then come and offer your gift. 25 Agree with your adversary quickly, while you are on the way with him, lest your adversary deliver you to the judge, the judge hand you over to the officer, and you be thrown into prison. 26 Assuredly, I say to you, you will by no means get out of there till you have paid the last penny."

7. The scribes and Pharisees had mandated that referring to someone as "Raca," or "empty-headed," provided just cause in court for a libel charge. But what warning does Jesus issue to help us understand the full impact of hateful words (see verses 21–22)?

8. Offering a gift at the temple as part of worship was considered a sacred act. How does Jesus use this pious act to emphasize the importance of reconciliation (see verses 23–26)?

REVIEWING THE STORY

John emphasizes that believers in Christ have undergone a profound change. Because of Jesus' sacrificial death and resurrection, and our acceptance of Him as Savior, we have passed from death to eternal life. This change must be reflected in the way we live—specifically, in the way we interact with others. God calls us to demonstrate sacrificial love. We must set aside the emotions, prejudices, and issues that cause divisiveness and seek the best for others, regardless of how it affects us. God blesses us richly when we back up our words of love with actions.

9. How does the world react to those who truly belong to God (see 1 John 3:13–15)?

10. How can we imitate Christ in our interactions with other people (see 1 John 3:16–17)?

11. How will people know our faith is genuine (see 1 John 3:18–19)?

12. How can we be confident when we approach God in prayer (see 1 John 3:21–24)?

APPLYING THE MESSAGE

13. What triggers do you need to avoid in order to better maintain a loving attitude?

_____

_____

_____

_____

_____

_____

_____

14. What do you want people to take away from their encounters with you?

_____

_____

_____

_____

_____

_____

_____

REFLECTING ON THE MEANING

John's stresses in this section that hatred is not an option for followers of Christ. Those who have accepted Jesus recognize the depth of the sacrifice that He made on their behalf—giving up his own life to atone for their sins. Such an act should cause us to pause when we are tempted to lash out against others and instead react in the way that Jesus demonstrated for us: through *love*. John offers three key insights in this passage to help guide our efforts.

First, *we must recognize the love we are called to share is not natural in this world*. John warns the believers not to marvel if the world hates them (see 1 John 3:12). Often, the world will respond to our higher calling by labeling it hypocrisy and scrutinizing us for cracks in the facade. This gives us an opportunity to subvert expectations and catch people off guard. Genuine love—the kind that doesn't call attention to itself or wrap itself in false piety—can make a huge impact on not only those who are directly affected by it, but also on others who witness it or hear about it later. Every interaction gives us an opportunity to confirm or dispel the world's opinion of us. We need to embrace the opportunity to defy stereotypes.

Second, *we must recognize that the kind of love God wants us to demonstrate will require some form of sacrifice*. John writes that we should be willing to "lay down our lives for the brethren" (verse 16). Our acts of love will likely not involve us laying down our lives for another person, as Jesus did for us, but there will be a sacrifice involved. This may take the form of us sacrificing our time, our energy, and our resources to help others. But there are more difficult things we will be required to sacrifice as well—such as our pride, our stubbornness, and our desire to "win" and "be right" at any cost. If we give up these divisive attitudes and motivators, we will find that people are more open to hearing what we have to say.

Third, *we must recognize that we have all the resources we need to fulfill God's command to love others*. John emphasizes that "whatever we ask we receive from [God], because we keep His commandments and do those things that are pleasing in His sight" (verse 22). God knows our hearts. If our goal is truly to obey His command and show love to others, then He will equip and prepare us for the task. All we have to do is ask.

By recognizing these truths, we will find that it is easier for us to love others. We will not always get it perfect in this life, but we can know that God will reward our efforts when our heart's desire to serve Him. As we do, we will also find that we are becoming more like Christ.

JOURNALING YOUR RESPONSE

What are you willing to sacrifice for the sake of loving others as Christ did?

LOVING GOD—LOVING EACH OTHER

1 John 4:1–11

GETTING STARTED

How has understanding God's love toward you helped you to better love the people in your life?

_____

_____

_____

_____

_____

_____

_____

_____

_____

_____

_____

SETTING THE STAGE

Jerome, an early church father, recorded an interesting story about the disciple John that took place in his later years. The apostle was frail, so his disciples would carry him into the gathering of believers. Each week, his words to the members were, "Little children, love one another." This went on week after week after week, until the congregation grew weary of his repeated phrase. Finally, one of John's disciples asked, "Master, why do you always say this?" John responded, "Because it is the Lord's command, and if only this is done, it is enough."

We cannot know for sure if this story is fact or fiction, but it does capture the heart of John in his first letter. In fact, for the apostle it seems that if the Christian life could be boiled down to just one word, that word would be *love*. But with so many other spiritual truths in the Bible, why does love play such a role? Why does the word *love* appear more than thirty times in John's three letters? Why does the beloved disciple make it the focus of all his correspondence?

The answer is that love begins with *God*. The reason that God's love plays such a prominent role in Scripture is because it is so extraordinary, so unlikely, and so undeserved. Because we chose to break our relationship with Him, there is no obligation on God's part for Him to love us. Yet He does—and that realization calls for action on our part.

John's point in this next section is that we are not created to be mere receptacles of God's love. Instead, we're called to be conduits, or channels, for directing God's love outward to others. We receive His love in our lives so that we can pass it on to others. This is the win-win scenario that John envisions: everyone experiencing God's love.

EXPLORING THE TEXT

Love for God and One Another (1 John 4:1–6)

¹ Beloved, do not believe every spirit, but test the spirits, whether they are of God; because many false prophets have gone out into the world. ² By this you know the Spirit of God: Every spirit that confesses that Jesus Christ has come in the flesh is of God, ³ and every spirit that does not confess that Jesus Christ has come in the flesh is not

of God. And this is the spirit of the Antichrist, which you have heard was coming, and is now already in the world.

⁴ You are of God, little children, and have overcome them, because He who is in you is greater than he who is in the world. ⁵ They are of the world. Therefore they speak as of the world, and the world hears them. ⁶ We are of God. He who knows God hears us; he who is not of God does not hear us. By this we know the spirit of truth and the spirit of error.

---

1. John has just stated it is the Holy Spirit's presence in a believer's life that confirms his or her relationship with God (see 1 John 3:24). But this raises an issue, for a false teacher could claim (and were claiming) that they were speaking by the Holy Spirit's guidance. What tests does John propose to ensure a person is speaking God's truths (see verses 1–3)?

2. John perceives the battle between believers in Christ and the "antichrists" as a struggle between good and evil. However, those who abide with Christ can be assured of victory. What assurance does John provide of this truth (see verses 4–6)?

Knowing God Through Love (1 John 4:7–11)

> [7] Beloved, let us love one another, for love is of God; and everyone who loves is born of God and knows God. [8] He who does not love does not know God, for God is love. [9] In this the love of God was manifested toward us, that God has sent His only begotten Son into the world, that we might live through Him. [10] In this is love, not that we loved God, but that He loved us and sent His Son to be the propitiation for our sins. [11] Beloved, if God so loved us, we also ought to love one another.

3. John has just noted that those who are speaking God's truths will have sound doctrine. They will confess that "Jesus Christ has come in the flesh" and not seek to distort the gospel. However, truth is just one side of the equation. What is another way that the believers can know whether a person is of God and speaking His words (see verses 7–8)?

4. John next describes the kind of love that proves God is present in a person's life. What kind of love did God show toward us? How are we to respond to that action (see verses 9–10)

_____

_____

_____

_____

_____

_____

_____

_____

_____

_____

GOING DEEPER

As we have seen, John's primary motive for writing this letter was to expose false teachers who were preaching a gospel that was contrary to the one the believers had received from him. For John, only those teachers who spoke the true gospel they had received were of God and operating in the power of the Holy Spirit. Jesus made a similar claim to His disciples. In the following passage, He reveals how the Holy Spirit will guide His followers in truth.

The Work of the Holy Spirit (John 16:7–15)

7 "Nevertheless I tell you the truth. It is to your advantage that I go away; for if I do not go away, the Helper will not come to you; but if I depart, I will send Him to you. 8 And when He has come, He will convict the world of sin, and of righteousness, and of judgment: 9 of sin, because they do not believe in Me; 10 of righteousness, because I go to My Father and you see Me no more; 11 of judgment, because the ruler of this world is judged.

¹² "I still have many things to say to you, but you cannot bear them now. ¹³ However, when He, the Spirit of truth, has come, He will guide you into all truth; for He will not speak on His own authority, but whatever He hears He will speak; and He will tell you things to come. ¹⁴ He will glorify Me, for He will take of what is Mine and declare it to you. ¹⁵ All things that the Father has are Mine. Therefore I said that He will take of Mine and declare it to you."

---

5. Jesus spoke these words to the disciples as He prepared them for His departure from the earth. The disciples certainly wondered how it could be to their advantage for Jesus to go away. But what does Jesus say that the Holy Spirit will do for them (see verses 7–11)?

6. The Holy Spirit has the role of convicting people of what is right and wrong and what is true and false. How could the disciples know whether a person is truly speaking words inspired by the Holy Spirit? What will the Holy Spirit always do (see verses 12–15)?

For John, speaking sound doctrine was just one proof of whether a person was operating in the power of the Holy Spirit. A second test was whether the person was genuinely reflecting God's love to others. The apostle Paul, in his letter to the church in Ephesus, also emphasizes this point and offers some specifics about what sharing God's love looks like in daily life.

Do Not Grieve the Spirit (Ephesians 4:25–32)

[25] Therefore, putting away lying, "Let each one of you speak truth with his neighbor," for we are members of one another. [26] "Be angry, and do not sin": do not let the sun go down on your wrath, [27] nor give place to the devil. [28] Let him who stole steal no longer, but rather let him labor, working with his hands what is good, that he may have something to give him who has need. [29] Let no corrupt word proceed out of your mouth, but what is good for necessary edification, that it may impart grace to the hearers. [30] And do not grieve the Holy Spirit of God, by whom you were sealed for the day of redemption. [31] Let all bitterness, wrath, anger, clamor, and evil speaking be put away from you, with all malice. [32] And be kind to one another, tenderhearted, forgiving one another, even as God in Christ forgave you.

7. The apotstle Paul emphasizes that lying, stealing, saying corrupt words, and speaking out of anger are not loving actions that we should be taking toward our fellow believers in Christ. What instructions does he instead offer for maintaining a loving spirit (see verses 25–29)?

_____

_____

_____

_____

_____

_____

8. We are not to grieve the Holy Spirit through our unloving actions but to remember that God extended His grace to us and forgave us even while we were still His enemies. How should that truth influence the attitude we take toward other people (see verses 30–32)?

_____

_____

_____

_____

_____

_____

REVIEWING THE STORY

John warns his readers about false teachers who are leading people astray. He urges them to not accept anyone at face value but to carefully examine their teachings and lives for evidence of God's loving transformation. If such evidence is not there, the teaching is "antichrist" and must be rejected. John also contrasts these teachers' worldliness with true Christian lovingkindness. He reminds the believers of the sacrifice that God made in sending His Son to die for their sins—citing it as the ultimate demonstration of God's love. John concluded by that stating that anyone who genuinely experiences God's love will naturally pass it on to others.

9. Why does John warn believers to "test the spirits" (1 John 4:1)?

_____

_____

_____

_____

_____

_____

10. How can we recognize the spirit of truth (see 1 John 4:4–6)?

11. What reason does John give for Christians to love one another (see 1 John 4:7–8)?

12. Why did God choose to send His Son into the world (see 1 John 4:9)?

APPLYING THE MESSAGE

13. What steps do you take to discern whether something is truly from God?

_____

_____

_____

_____

_____

14. What are some truths that God has revealed to you recently in His Word?

_____

_____

_____

_____

_____

_____

REFLECTING ON THE MEANING

In this section of John's letter, he makes a statement that would have been surprising to the people of his day: "God is love" (1 John 4:8). In the pagan religions of John's time, the gods were not portrayed as being personal, giving, or agreeable, let alone _loving_. But here John states that God—_the_ God—does not merely love but actually _is_ love. Furthermore, when we open the pages of the Bible, we discover that God's love is like a multi-faced diamond, with each of its many sides revealing something unique about its overall beauty.

First, God's love is uncaused. The world places conditions on love. "I love you if you are good-looking, intelligent, wealthy, and have a good job and strong connections." There are endless *ifs* and conditions hidden in the world's love. But God's love for us is unprompted and uninfluenced. It is free and spontaneous. There is nothing we can do to cause God to love us, and there is nothing that we can do to prevent Him from loving us. As Paul wrote, God simply loves us "according to the good pleasure of His will" (Ephesians 1:5).

Second, God's love is unending. We divide time into past, present, and future, but God sees beyond those divisions. He "inhabits eternity" (Isaiah 57:15) and is "the King eternal" (1 Timothy 1:17). Therefore, since God is eternal, and God is love, it only follows that His love is eternal. The love He will have for us in the future will never be greater than the love He has for us right now. The prophet Jeremiah put it this way: "Yes, I have loved you with an everlasting love; therefore with loving-kindness I have drawn you" (Jeremiah 31:3).

Third, God's love is unchanging. In a mordern world that is fast-paced and ever-changing, we can be assured of one simple truth: the character of God never changes. As the Lord said to His people, "I am the LORD, I do not change" (Malachi 3:6). Given this reality that God Himself never changes, it only stands to reason that His love for us also never changes. There is only a good side and a better side to God's unchanging love. The good side is that God won't wake up in the morning and decide that He has had enough of us. The better side is that even when *we* wake up in the morning and decide we've had enough of Him, He still chooses to love us.

It is for these reasons that the apostle John could state that "God is love" (1 John 4:8), and our response to such love must be to "love one another" (verse 11). Now, you may be wondering, *Lord, are You really asking me to love so-and-so?* The answer is, "Yes!" But not in your own strength. If you will meditate on God's unconditional, sacrificial, and personal love for you, you will find new reasons and new resources for loving even those unlovable people in your life.

JOURNALING YOUR RESPONSE

What do you want people to most see in the way you interact with others?

CASTING OUT FEAR

1 John 4:12–21

GETTING STARTED

What is one fear in your life that you would most like to overcome?

_____

_____

_____

_____

_____

_____

_____

_____

_____

_____

_____

_____

_____

_____

_____

SETTING THE STAGE

The apostle John has been building his arguments as to why it is so critical for believers in Christ to receive God's love and also express that same love to others. As he closes his words on this subject, he calls out one final benefit of abiding in God's love: *it casts out fear.* In John's words, "There is no fear in love; but perfect love casts out fear, because fear involves torment. But he who fears has not been made perfect in love" (1 John 4:18).

Many people live in fear today. Often, humanly speaking, there is good reason for this fear. Terrorism, unprecedented natural disasters, wars, economic downturns, disease, and the normal ups and downs of life threaten communities across the world. As a result, many live with a free-floating sense of worry—a general feeling that something is wrong or about to go wrong. Instead of waking up every morning with a sense of faith-based optimism, they greet the day hoping that God will protect them from whatever happens.

Free-floating worry affects many in our world—and many in our churches. Even Christians are not exempt from this low-grade fear of life. This is why John encourages each of us to abide in God's love and recognize the status that we have been given as His children. When we do this, we understand that God is as pleased with us as He is with His own Son. We realize that He is watching over us and that His plans and purposes will not be thwarted by the events of life. As we walk in this awareness, our fear is replaced by confidence.

Jesus feared nothing in this life because of the love between Him and His Father. In the same way, Christians who walk in the love of God fear neither dictators nor disasters nor disease nor death. They have peace because of their confidence that God loves them—and they know nothing can separate them from that love.

Exploring the Text

Seeing God Through Love (1 John 4:12–16)

> [12] No one has seen God at any time. If we love one another, God abides in us, and His love has been perfected in us. [13] By this we know that we abide in Him, and He in us, because He has given us

of His Spirit. ¹⁴ And we have seen and testify that the Father has sent the Son as Savior of the world. ¹⁵ Whoever confesses that Jesus is the Son of God, God abides in him, and he in God. ¹⁶ And we have known and believed the love that God has for us. God is love, and he who abides in love abides in God, and God in him.

---

1. John opens this section of his letter with the statement that "no one has seen God." Even though none of us can see God, how does John say that we can know for sure that God is abiding in us? What happens as we do this (see verses 12–13)?

_____

_____

_____

_____

_____

_____

_____

2. John follows up his comment that "no one has seen God" with a statement of what he has personally seen: God the Father sent His Son into the world to redeem humanity from sin. What does John say about those who make this same confession? What does he say is true for those who choose to abide in the love of God (see verses 14–16)?

_____

_____

_____

_____

_____

_____

_____

The Consummation of Love (1 John 4:17–21)

¹⁷ Love has been perfected among us in this: that we may have boldness in the day of judgment; because as He is, so are we in this world. ¹⁸ There is no fear in love; but perfect love casts out fear, because fear involves torment. But he who fears has not been made perfect in love. ¹⁹ We love Him because He first loved us.

²⁰ If someone says, "I love God," and hates his brother, he is a liar; for he who does not love his brother whom he has seen, how can he love God whom he has not seen? ²¹ And this commandment we have from Him: that he who loves God must love his brother also.

3. John has just stated that "if we love one another, God abides in us, and His love has been perfected in us" (verse 12). He will now expound on how we can know God's love has been perfected in us. What does John say our attitude will be if we are abiding in God's perfect love? What will our attitude be if we are not (see verses 17–18)?

4. Our love is based on the example of love we have received from God. Given this, why is it impossible for us to say we love God while harboring hatred or resentment toward another person? What is God's command to us in this regard (see verses 19–21)?

_____

_____

_____

_____

_____

_____

_____

_____

_____

_____

_____

_____

GOING DEEPER

In the Gospel of John, we likewise find Jesus teaching His followers about the benefits of abiding in Him and the impact it should have on our confidence before God. In the following passages, Jesus first uses the analogy of a vine and branches to reveal the way in which we should be depending on God. He then explains that those who have received God's love and accepted His salvation have nothing to fear on the coming day of judgment.

The True Vine (John 15:4–8)

⁴ "Abide in Me, and I in you. As the branch cannot bear fruit of itself, unless it abides in the vine, neither can you, unless you abide in Me.

⁵ "I am the vine, you are the branches. He who abides in Me, and I in him, bears much fruit; for without Me you can do nothing.

⁶ If anyone does not abide in Me, he is cast out as a branch and is withered; and they gather them and throw them into the fire, and they are burned. ⁷ If you abide in Me, and My words abide in you, you will ask what you desire, and it shall be done for you. ⁸ By this My Father is glorified, that you bear much fruit; so you will be My disciples."

---

5. Jesus explains that for a branch to produce fruit, it must abide—or sink deeper—into the vine for strength. How does this apply to believers in Christ (see verses 4–5)?

_____

_____

_____

_____

_____

_____

_____

_____

6. A loss of fellowship (being "cast out"), a loss of vitality (being "withered"), and a loss of reward (being "burned") are real consequences for those who neglect their relationship with Christ. In contrast, what can we expect if we abide in Christ (see verses 6–8)?

_____

_____

_____

_____

_____

_____

_____

_____

Jesus Christ Has Overcome the World (John 16:25–33)

²⁵ "These things I have spoken to you in figurative language; but the time is coming when I will no longer speak to you in figurative language, but I will tell you plainly about the Father. ²⁶ In that day you will ask in My name, and I do not say to you that I shall pray the Father for you; ²⁷ for the Father Himself loves you, because you have loved Me, and have believed that I came forth from God. ²⁸ I came forth from the Father and have come into the world. Again, I leave the world and go to the Father."

²⁹ His disciples said to Him, "See, now You are speaking plainly, and using no figure of speech! ³⁰ Now we are sure that You know all things, and have no need that anyone should question You. By this we believe that You came forth from God."

³¹ Jesus answered them, "Do you now believe? ³² Indeed the hour is coming, yes, has now come, that you will be scattered, each to his own, and will leave Me alone. And yet I am not alone, because the Father is with Me. ³³ These things I have spoken to you, that in Me you may have peace. In the world you will have tribulation; but be of good cheer, I have overcome the world."

7. Jesus tells His disciples that they are not to regard Him as an intermediary who is encouraging a reluctant God to answer their prayers. What privilege and access to God have they been given because of their abiding relationship with Christ (see verses 25–28)?

_____

_____

_____

_____

_____

_____

_____

8. Jesus applauds the disciples' belief but states that an hour is coming when they will scatter. What does Jesus say to encourage them through this time (see verses 31–33)?

_____

_____

_____

_____

_____

_____

REVIEWING THE STORY

The apostle John explains the connection between loving one another, abiding in God, and having His love perfected in us. The presence of the Holy Spirit in our lives confirms our abiding relationship with God. Anyone who confesses that Jesus is the Son of God may enjoy the untold blessings that come with the relationship. Chief among them is the freedom from fear. Believers have no reason to fear God's judgment— or anything else, for that matter. God's perfect love drives out fear. That same love compels us to love others.

9. How do we know that God abides in us (see 1 John 4:12)?

_____

_____

_____

_____

_____

_____

10. How do we know that we abide in God (see 1 John 4:13)?

11. Why are believers able to have "boldness in the day of judgment" (1 John 4:17)?

12. What does God's perfect love do (see 1 John 4:18)?

APPLYING THE MESSAGE

13. What does boldness look like in your relationship with God?

_____

_____

_____

_____

_____

_____

_____

_____

_____

_____

14. How can you keep fear from disrupting that relationship?

_____

_____

_____

_____

_____

_____

_____

_____

_____

REFLECTING ON THE MEANING

"There is no fear in love . . . perfect love casts out fear" (1 John 4:18). The whole of Scripture can be summarized under the heading of God's love for humankind. Everywhere we look in the Bible, we find evidence that God's love will enable us to overcome all types of fear.

First, God's love protects us from the fear of discouragement. God is in the picture in every passage of Scripture that exhorts us not to be dismayed or discouraged. For example, in Deuteronomy 31:8, Moses assured the Israelites that God would be with them as they crossed over the Jordan into the Promised Land. In 1 Chronicles 28:20, David encouraged his son Solomon with the promise of the Lord's presence. When God is present, there's no reason to be discouraged. He's already proven His love for us by giving us His Son. Won't He give us everything else we need, including His encouragement?

Second, God's love protects us from the fear of danger and even death. The prophet Isaiah wrote, "Behold, God is my salvation, I will trust and not be afraid . . . the LORD, is my strength and song; He has also become my salvation" (12:2). Faith in God's love isn't only like a medicine we take whenever we "come down" with fear. It is also like a vaccine we receive that protects us from fear. Furthermore, in Hebrews 2:14–15, we read that Christ destroyed "him who had the power of death" so that "those who through fear of death were all their lifetime subject to bondage" might be set free. We don't have to fear death because we trust in the promise that Christ has secured for us the gift of eternal life.

Third, God's love protects us from the fear of damnation. God's love gives us "boldness in the day of judgment" (1 John 4:17). We are instructed to have "the fear of the LORD" (Proverbs 1:7), but this is not a cowering fear. Rather we are to have an awe and reverence in God's presence—a worshipful response to His great love. This fear of God keeps us from fearing His judgment. We know that His love is responsible for Christ having been judged in our place. As a result, we have no fear of judgment leading to damnation.

God promises that we can confidently abide in His love. As we do this—walking in His ways and sharing His love—we will experience His love being perfected in us. And when God's love is perfected in us, we will discover that we have nothing to fear in this life or the next.

JOURNALING YOUR RESPONSE

How would your life look different if you operated more out of boldness than fear?

COMMANDMENT KEEPERS

1 John 5:1–10

GETTING STARTED

How have you experienced the Holy Spirit help you keep God's commands?

_____

_____

_____

_____

_____

_____

_____

_____

_____

_____

_____

_____

_____

_____

_____

_____

_____

_____

_____

_____

_____

SETTING THE STAGE

"I know you can do it" may be the six most inspirational words a person can say for the benefit of another. Under the right circumstances, these words can spur someone on to incredible accomplishments. Even better, they can leave a lasting impression on that person's life. We may not always be able to see the full extent of our own potential. So, when a respected person in our life encourages us to tap into some previously unrecognized reservoir of potential, it can forever change the way we look at our limitations and capabilities.

This I-know-you-can-do-it sensibility winds its way throughout this final section of John's first letter as he encourages the believers to keep God's commandments. John's words reveal a heartwarming truth about our heavenly Father: He has a higher opinion of us, and our ability to succeed, than we do of ourselves. Sometimes we view God's commandments through the lens of our human frailty, seeing expectations that are beyond us and convincing ourselves that only heroes of the faith can live the way God intends. We don't see a hero when we look in the mirror. We dwell on the pain and embarrassment of past failures. We sabotage ourselves.

But through it all, God's Holy Spirit speaks this truth to our hearts: *I know you can do it*. God knows exactly what we are made of because He put it there within us! He wants us to understand that living a life that is pleasing to Him is within our reach. He also wants us to recognize that His commandments are not a list of rules to be obeyed. Instead, they are a blueprint for living a fulfilling and difference-making life.

EXPLORING THE TEXT

Obedience by Faith (1 John 5:1–5)

---

¹ Whoever believes that Jesus is the Christ is born of God, and everyone who loves Him who begot also loves him who is begotten of Him. ² By this we know that we love the children of God, when

we love God and keep His commandments. ³ For this is the love of God, that we keep His commandments. And His commandments are not burdensome. ⁴ For whatever is born of God overcomes the world. And this is the victory that has overcome the world—our faith. ⁵ Who is he who overcomes the world, but he who believes that Jesus is the Son of God?

---

1. Notice that the apostle John, quite true to form in the letter, opens this section with a doctrinal test: "*Whoever* believes that Jesus is the Christ . . . *is* born of God" (verse 1). What other tests does John set forth for identifying true believers in Christ (see verses 1–2)?

_____

_____

_____

_____

_____

_____

2. Jesus once encouraged His followers, "Take My yoke upon you . . . for My yoke is easy and My burden is light" (Matthew 11:29–30). John emphasizes this same point by stressing that "[God's] commandments are not burdensome" (1 John 5:3), for those who have a relationship with God receive a new nature and *want* to keep His commands. What does this new nature also give us the power to do (see verses 3–5)?

_____

_____

_____

_____

_____

_____

The Certainty of God's Witness (1 John 5:6–10)

⁶ This is He who came by water and blood—Jesus Christ; not only by water, but by water and blood. And it is the Spirit who bears witness, because the Spirit is truth. ⁷ For there are three that bear witness in heaven: the Father, the Word, and the Holy Spirit; and these three are one. ⁸ And there are three that bear witness on earth: the Spirit, the water, and the blood; and these three agree as one.

⁹ If we receive the witness of men, the witness of God is greater; for this is the witness of God which He has testified of His Son. ¹⁰ He who believes in the Son of God has the witness in himself; he who does not believe God has made Him a liar, because he has not believed the testimony that God has given of His Son.

3. John's statement that Jesus came "not only by water, but by water and blood" (verse 6), seems at first glance to be an unnecessary detail about Christ's mission on earth. However, the point that John is making is that Jesus was both human (born by "blood") and divine (born by "water" or the Holy Spirit). This is important because certain false teachers were claiming that Jesus was *only* human or *only* divine. Who does John say bears witness to this truth in heaven? Who bears witness to this truth on earth (see verses 6–8)?

4. John uses the concept of "the witness" to contrast a person who accepts what God says and a person who rejects what God says. What does John say that a person who rejects God's testimony about His Son is actually doing (see verses 9–10)?

_____

_____

_____

_____

_____

_____

_____

_____

GOING DEEPER

In this section, John spells out what it means for us to choose the life that God offers instead of the life that the world offers. In the book of Deuteronomy, we read of a similar choice that Moses offered the people of Israel. In both cases, making the choice to receive God's life requires an action on our part: we must choose to follow God's commands.

The Choice of Life or Death (Deuteronomy 30:11–16)

¹¹ "For this commandment which I command you today is not too mysterious for you, nor is it far off. ¹² It is not in heaven, that you should say, 'Who will ascend into heaven for us and bring it to us, that we may hear it and do it?' ¹³ Nor is it beyond the sea, that you should say, 'Who will go over the sea for us and bring it to us, that we may hear it and do it?' ¹⁴ But the word is very near you, in your mouth and in your heart, that you may do it.

¹⁵ "See, I have set before you today life and good, death and evil, ¹⁶ in that I command you today to love the LORD your God, to walk

in His ways, and to keep His commandments, His statutes, and His judgments, that you may live and multiply; and the LORD your God will bless you in the land which you go to possess."

---

5. Moses tells the Israelite people that God's commands are "not too mysterious" for them, just as the apostle John tells the believers that God's commands "are not burdensome" for them to keep. Something that is "mysterious" or "far off" may be difficult to understand or carry out successfully. Why are God's commandments not too difficult to obey (verses 11–14)?

_____

_____

_____

_____

_____

_____

_____

6. The challenge that Moses presented to the Israelites was for them to follow God's commands so they would receive "life and good" rather than "death and evil." What incentive does he add that they will receive when they obey God (see verses 15–16)?

_____

_____

_____

_____

_____

_____

In the Gospels, we discover that even Jesus had to make the choice to obey God's will. On the night before His crucifixion, He went to the Garden of Gethsemane to prepare for His death by spending time with His Father. As the following passage relates, Jesus once and for all proved Himself to be a commandment keeper and set an enduring example for His followers.

The Prayer in the Garden (Luke 22:39–44)

[39] Coming out, He went to the Mount of Olives, as He was accustomed, and His disciples also followed Him. [40] When He came to the place, He said to them, "Pray that you may not enter into temptation."

[41] And He was withdrawn from them about a stone's throw, and He knelt down and prayed, [42] saying, "Father, if it is Your will, take this cup away from Me; nevertheless not My will, but Yours, be done." [43] Then an angel appeared to Him from heaven, strengthening Him. [44] And being in agony, He prayed more earnestly. Then His sweat became like great drops of blood falling down to the ground.

7. What request did Jesus make of His disciples when they entered into the Garden? Why do you think Christ asked them to do this (see verses 39–40)?

8. What request did Jesus make of His heavenly Father? How did He prove in this instance that he loved God and was willing to obey His commands (see verses 41–44)?

_____

_____

_____

_____

_____

_____

REVIEWING THE STORY

True love for God is marked not only by a love for His people but also by obedience to His Word. For John, the connection is a simple one—those who truly love God will want to show that love by following God's commands. Furthermore, these commands are not oppressive but lead to freedom, happiness, and victory. In fact, the only ones who are able to overcome the world are those who believe that Jesus is the Son of God. To bolster that belief, John reminds us that three unimpeachable witnesses testify to Jesus' identity as God's Son: the Father, the Word of God, and the Holy Spirit. These three agree together as one.

9. How does John summarize what it means to love God (see 1 John 5:3)?

_____

_____

_____

_____

_____

_____

10. Of what victory are we assured if we are born of God (see 1 John 5:4–5)?

11. What two things marked Jesus' coming (see 1 John 5:6)?

12. Why can we trust the testimony of the Holy Spirit (see 1 John 5:6)?

APPLYING THE MESSAGE

13. What are some commands from God that have seemed burdensome to you in the past?

_____

_____

_____

_____

_____

_____

_____

_____

_____

_____

14. What benefits did you receive when you followed those commands out of your love for God—in spite of how you may have been feeling?

_____

_____

_____

_____

_____

_____

_____

_____

_____

_____

_____

_____

REFLECTING ON THE MEANING

"By this we know that we love the children of God, when we love God and keep His commandments. For this is the love of God, that we keep His commandments" (1 John 5:2–3). These statements from the apostle John leave no room for compromise. They are similar to the *if/then* conditions that he has employed throughout his epistle for determining the true believer from the false. *If* we say we love God . . . *then* we will keep His commands.

We face the test of keeping God's commands every day. Especially when it comes to dealing with other people. *Pray for our enemies? Turn the other cheek? Do good to those who hate us?* Commands such as these push us out of our comfort zones because, humanly speaking, they do not come naturally. We would rather ask God to punish our enemies. Return the slap on our cheek with a cutting remark. Do anything but *good* to those who hate us.

How can we hope to follow these commands? We do so by recognizing the connection between loving God and obeying Him. Jesus had told His followers, "If you love Me, keep My commandments" (John 14:15). The disciple John likely had this in mind when he penned his instructions to his readers. Simply put, love for God will reveal itself in *obedience*.

Think of this in terms of a parent-and-child relationship. Good parents set rules for their children out of their love for them. They want to protect their children and see them grow into adults, so they set guidelines to keep them safe and on the right track. Children obey these rules not just because they fear the consequences if they do not, but also because they love their parents and do not want to displease them. It is a two-way relationship.

When we view obeying God in this manner—as an act of love for Him just as a child loves a parent—we find that "His commands are not burdensome" (1 John 5:3). We recognize that God's laws are *gifts* from Him that show us the best life possible. We desire to please Him because we have been born again and given new hearts that desire His ways. *If* we say we love God in this way . . . *then* we will naturally want to keep His commands.

JOURNALING YOUR RESPONSE

What practical step can you take today to help you grow in your relationship with God?

ASSURANCE OF SALVATION

1 John 5:11–21

GETTING STARTED

What were the circumstances that led to your salvation?

_____

_____

_____

_____

_____

_____

_____

_____

_____

_____

_____

_____

_____

_____

_____

_____

_____

_____

_____

_____

_____

_____

SETTING THE STAGE

One of the most-asked questions that church leaders receive is, "How can I know that I'm saved?" The question usually comes from those who have identified as Christians for most of their lives. Perhaps they had a faith experience when they were young, but over the years, doubts have crept into their hearts. Or perhaps they allowed sin to take root and now they doubt if they were saved in the first place. Or maybe they question whether they prayed the right prayer, or said the right words, and so their salvation doesn't seem "official."

Whatever the cause of the doubts, the results can be devastating. After all, if we are not sure of our own salvation, why would we ever want to share our faith with someone else? Why would we want to go to church, where the sermons make us feel worse and the worship leaves us feeling empty? Why would we want to read the Bible, which only makes us feel more condemned and more distant from God?

The authors of the New Testament frequently dealt with this issue of knowing what we believe and being sure of our relationship with Christ. But the apostle John writes about it more than any other New Testament writer. Two of his five books deal specifically with salvation: his Gospel and this first letter. In fact, at the end of 1 John, we read these words: "These things I have written to you who believe in the name of the Son of God, that you may know that you have eternal life, and that you may continue to believe in the name of the Son of God" (5:13). This is the message that we will be exploring as we wrap up our study of this letter.

EXPLORING THE TEXT

Confidence and Compassion in Prayer (1 John 5:11–17)

> ¹¹ And this is the testimony: that God has given us eternal life, and this life is in His Son. ¹² He who has the Son has life; he who does not have the Son of God does not have life. ¹³ These things I have

written to you who believe in the name of the Son of God, that you may know that you have eternal life, and that you may continue to believe in the name of the Son of God.

¹⁴ Now this is the confidence that we have in Him, that if we ask anything according to His will, He hears us. ¹⁵ And if we know that He hears us, whatever we ask, we know that we have the petitions that we have asked of Him.

¹⁶ If anyone sees his brother sinning a sin which does not lead to death, he will ask, and He will give him life for those who commit sin not leading to death. There is sin leading to death. I do not say that he should pray about that. ¹⁷ All unrighteousness is sin, and there is sin not leading to death.

---

1. John comes to the conclusion of his letter with a summary of the gospel: "He who has the Son has life" (verse 12). What does John then add is the purpose of his writing? What assurance does he want his readers to have (see verses 11–13)?

_____

_____

_____

_____

_____

_____

_____

_____

_____

_____

2. John now summarizes the privileges that true believers receive as it relates to their prayers. What promises do believers have as it relates to their prayers for themselves? What promises are they given as it relates to their prayers for others (see verses 14–17)?

_____

_____

_____

_____

_____

Knowing the True—Rejecting the False (1 John 5:18–21)

18 We know that whoever is born of God does not sin; but he who has been born of God keep himself, and the wicked one does not touch him.

19 We know that we are of God, and the whole world lies under the sway of the wicked one.

20 And we know that the Son of God has come and has given us an understanding, that we may know Him who is true; and we are in Him who is true, in His Son Jesus Christ. This is the true God and eternal life.

21 Little children, keep yourselves from idols. Amen.

3. John closes his letter with three absolute truths, each of which begins with the phrase, "we know." What does John want his readers to remember with unshakable certainty as it relates to their place in the world and the attacks of the enemy (see verses 18–19)?

_____

_____

_____

_____

_____

_____

4. What does John want his readers to remember with unshakable certainty as it relates to what the Son of God has done in their lives (see verses 18–21)?

_____

_____

_____

_____

_____

_____

_____

_____

_____

_____

GOING DEEPER

The question of how a person can be assured of salvation is at the heart of the gospel. As we have seen, the apostle John wrote this epistle so that his readers would _know_ that they have eternal life. Jesus likewise instructed His followers on how they could be assured of their salvation, as the following passages from the Gospel of John relate.

The Bread of Life (John 6:43–51)

43 Jesus therefore answered and said to them, "Do not murmur among yourselves. 44 No one can come to Me unless the Father who sent Me draws him; and I will raise him up at the last day. 45 It is written in the prophets, 'And they shall all be taught by God.' Therefore everyone who has heard and learned from the Father comes to Me. 46 Not that anyone has seen the Father, except He who is from God; He has seen the Father. 47 Most assuredly, I say to you, he who believes

in Me has everlasting life. ⁴⁸ I am the bread of life. ⁴⁹ Your fathers ate the manna in the wilderness, and are dead. ⁵⁰ This is the bread which comes down from heaven, that one may eat of it and not die. ⁵¹ I am the living bread which came down from heaven. If anyone eats of this bread, he will live forever; and the bread that I shall give is My flesh, which I shall give for the life of the world."

---

5. Jesus spoke these words in response to "murmur" from the Jewish religious leaders that He was claiming to be the divine Son of God rather than the human son of Joseph. How did Jesus respond to their complaint? What did He say about Himself (see verses 43–46)?

_____

_____

_____

_____

_____

_____

6. How did Jesus state that a person could be assured that he or she has eternal life? What does it mean to eat of the "living bread" that Jesus offers (see verses 47–51)?

_____

_____

_____

_____

_____

_____

_____

The Shepherd Knows His Sheep (John 10:22–30)

²² Now it was the Feast of Dedication in Jerusalem, and it was winter. ²³ And Jesus walked in the temple, in Solomon's porch. ²⁴ Then the Jews surrounded Him and said to Him, "How long do You keep us in doubt? If You are the Christ, tell us plainly."

²⁵ Jesus answered them, "I told you, and you do not believe. The works that I do in My Father's name, they bear witness of Me. ²⁶ But you do not believe, because you are not of My sheep, as I said to you. ²⁷ My sheep hear My voice, and I know them, and they follow Me. ²⁸ And I give them eternal life, and they shall never perish; neither shall anyone snatch them out of My hand. ²⁹ My Father, who has given them to Me, is greater than all; and no one is able to snatch them out of My Father's hand. ³⁰ I and My Father are one."

5. Jesus spoke these words in response to another challenge from the religious leaders about the claims that He was making. What answer did they demand of Him (see verses 22–24)?

_____

_____

_____

_____

_____

_____

_____

_____

_____

6. Jesus explains to the religious leaders that His works bear witness to the fact that He is the Son of God and that they do not recognize Him as such because they refuse to listen to God. What promise does Jesus give to those who *do* choose to hear His voice (see verses 25–30)?

_____

_____

_____

_____

_____

_____

_____

REVIEWING THE STORY

The apostle John ends his first letter by stating his reason for writing it. He wants the believers to be confident in their salvation so they will enjoy the full benefits of their relationship with God. These benefits include praying with the assurance that God will hear them, answer them, and work on behalf of those for whom they pray. John closes with three absolute truths: (1) whoever is born of God does not sin, (2) the world lies under the sway of the wicked one, and (3) the Son of God has come to bring eternal life. Finally, he issues a last command to his "little children" to encourage them to keep themselves from idols and the sinful ways of the world.

9. How does John summarize his testimony (see 1 John 5:11–12)?

_____

_____

_____

_____

_____

_____

_____

10. Who can be assured of eternal life (see 1 John 5:13)?

11. What happens when we are born of God (see 1 John 5:18)?

12. What understanding does the Son of God give to us
(see 1 John 5:20)?

Applying the Message

13. What are some of the doubts that you have wrestled with concerning your faith?

_____

_____

_____

_____

_____

_____

_____

14. How can you help someone else who is wrestling with doubts about his or her salvation?

_____

_____

_____

_____

_____

_____

_____

Reflecting on the Meaning

Five times in this short letter, the apostle John uses the term *born of God* or *begotten of God*. Each time he uses the term, he describes what it means to be born again, and in doing so, gives us a test or evidence of being born again. These instances might be referred to as the "birth marks" of the believer. Here are five such marks that provide assurance of our salvation.

First, *the birthmark of confession* (see 1 John 5:1). We can know that we are born again if we believe that Jesus is the Son of the living God. There are really two answers at our disposal if someone asks if we are a Christian. The first is to point to ourselves and outline everything we have done to be a Christian. Such a response indicates that we *have not* been born again. The second is to point to Christ and outline everything that He has done for us. This response is the evidence that we truly have received salvation—the mark of our confession of sins.

Second, *the birthmark of change* (see 1 John 2:29). John reminds us that if we say we are Christians, then we need to behave like we are Christians. This is not salvation by *doing* good works but salvation *demonstrated* by good works. If we truly desire to love and serve God, such a desire will manifest itself in a motivation to love and serve others.

Third, *the birthmark of compassion* (see 1 John 4:7). We can know that we are Christians by who we love. The apostle John writes that we love because God first loved us. So, if God loved us while we were yet sinners and invited us to be a part of His family, that act of mercy should compel us to reach out to others in their sin and compel them to be drawn into God's family.

Fourth, *the birthmark of conflict* (see 1 John 5:4). When we are born of God, we are overcomers in this world. We look to Jesus—the One who has gone before us and overcome the world—and draw strength from His victory. While we might not be victorious over every temptation, we can see that we are gaining more victories and losing fewer battles.

Fifth, *the birthmark of conduct* (see 1 John 5:18). When we sin as believers, and we are made aware of our sin, we come boldly before the throne of grace. We confess our sin, and ask God to forgive us, and then we forsake our sin. We may have to go through this many times with the very same sin, but we never just accept sin as a way of life.

Confession, change, compassion, conflict, and conduct. As we witness evidence of these birthmarks, we witness evidence that our salvation is secure in Christ. And when we are assured of our salvation, we receive the peace of God and the rest that He has promised to us.

JOURNALING YOUR RESPONSE

Which birthmark would you like to be more prominent in your life—
and why?

WALKING THE WALK

2 John 1:1–13

GETTING STARTED

How can you tell if someone "walks the walk" when it comes to his or her Christian faith?

_____

_____

_____

_____

_____

_____

_____

_____

_____

_____

_____

SETTING THE STAGE

In this age of social media, it's easy to present a false narrative of ourselves. By artfully crafting an online profile, we can make people believe we are someone we are not. We can cherry-pick family photos to make our parenting seem extraordinary. We can puff up our résumé to make our job seem more prestigious. We can quote the Bible and strategically drop humblebrags to make our ministry efforts seem more important. In other words, it's easier than ever these days to "talk the talk" without actually "walking the walk."

However, as John makes clear in his short second letter, it is not an option for true followers of Christ to talk the talk without walking the walk. In fact, a faith without the evidence of love and obedience to back it up cannot be a genuine faith. This was an especially important concept for the recipients of John's second letter to grasp. False teachers of a philosophy called "Docetism" had infiltrated the early churches. These deceivers were claiming that Jesus was not fully human—only divine. They were leading people astray with such lies.

So the beloved disciple did something extraordinary. The apostle who made love the central theme of most everything he wrote actually advised his readers to *withhold* their love and hospitality from the false teachers in their midst. The risks of associating with such people, even casually, was simply too great. God's rewards hung in the balance.

The same is true today. While the teachings may have changed, the danger of Christian deceivers is as real today as it was in John's day. For this reason, it is important for us to read his words and understand that we must "walk the walk" when it comes to our faith.

EXPLORING THE TEXT

Walk in Christ's Commandments (2 John 1:1–6)

[1] The Elder,

To the elect lady and her children, whom I love in truth, and not only I, but also all those who have known the truth, [2] because of the truth which abides in us and will be with us forever:

[3] Grace, mercy, and peace will be with you from God the Father and from the Lord Jesus Christ, the Son of the Father, in truth and love.

⁴ I rejoiced greatly that I have found some of your children walking in truth, as we received commandment from the Father. ⁵ And now I plead with you, lady, not as though I wrote a new commandment to you, but that which we have had from the beginning: that we love one another. ⁶ This is love, that we walk according to His commandments. This is the commandment, that as you have heard from the beginning, you should walk in it.

---

1. John addresses himself as "the Elder" in this letter, which implies that he held some form of authority in the church, and states that he is writing to "the elect lady and her children," which may literally refer to a biological family unit or figuratively to a church congregation. How does John address this group? What word does he stress in describing them (see verses 1–3)?

_____

_____

_____

_____

2. John's use of the phrase "walking in truth" refers to having an authentic relationship with God. How does walking in truth affect our relationships with other people (see verses 4–6)?

_____

_____

_____

Beware of Antichrist Deceivers (2 John 1:7–13)

⁷ For many deceivers have gone out into the world who do not confess Jesus Christ as coming in the flesh. This is a deceiver and an antichrist.

⁸ Look to yourselves, that we do not lose those things we worked for, but that we may receive a full reward.

⁹ Whoever transgresses and does not abide in the doctrine of Christ does not have God. He who abides in the doctrine of Christ has both the Father and the Son. ¹⁰ If anyone comes to you and does not bring this doctrine, do not receive him into your house nor greet him; ¹¹ for he who greets him shares in his evil deeds.

¹² Having many things to write to you, I did not wish to do so with paper and ink; but I hope to come to you and speak face to face, that our joy may be full.

¹³ The children of your elect sister greet you. Amen.

---

3. The apostle John now addresses his main concern in writing this letter. Jesus had told His followers that many would come "in [His] name" and would "deceive many" (Matthew 24:5). John sees this reality taking place, and so he warns this Christian community that "many deceivers have gone out into the world" (2 John 1:7). What were these false teachers proclaiming? What warning does John give regarding them (see verses 7–8)?

----

4. The Greek term that John uses for *greet* in this passage refers to identifying with a person publicly. How were the believers to treat those teachers who did not have sound doctrine? What is the consequence of associating with such individuals (see verses 10–11)?

GOING DEEPER

False teachers, deceivers, and divisive people pose a threat to spiritual growth. In the first-century church, they threatened to derail the work of Jesus' followers. Like John, the apostle Paul warned his congregations in Rome and Galatia that such people should not be tolerated.

Avoid Divisive Persons (Romans 16:17–20)

> 17 Now I urge you, brethren, note those who cause divisions and offenses, contrary to the doctrine which you learned, and avoid them. 18 For those who are such do not serve our Lord Jesus Christ, but their own belly, and by smooth words and flattering speech deceive the hearts of the simple. 19 For your obedience has become known to all. Therefore I am glad on your behalf; but I want you to be wise in what is good, and simple concerning evil. 20 And the God of peace will crush Satan under your feet shortly.
>
> The grace of our Lord Jesus Christ be with you. Amen.

5. The church in Rome was experiencing fissures in its fellowship. What is Paul's blunt advice regarding those who were causing "divisions and offenses" (see verses 17–18)?

6. Divisive people destroy peace and unity in the church. What happens when God's people show obedience and wisdom in responding to them (see verses 19–20)?

_____

_____

_____

_____

_____

_____

Obey the Truth (Galatians 5:7–12)

⁷ You ran well. Who hindered you from obeying the truth? ⁸ This persuasion does not come from Him who calls you. ⁹ A little leaven leavens the whole lump. ¹⁰ I have confidence in you, in the Lord, that you will have no other mind; but he who troubles you shall bear his judgment, whoever he is.

¹¹ And I, brethren, if I still preach circumcision, why do I still suffer persecution? Then the offense of the cross has ceased. ¹² I could wish that those who trouble you would even cut themselves off!

7. What question does the apostle Paul have for the believers in this community? What does he say about those who are causing divisions (see verses 7–8)?

_____

_____

_____

_____

_____

8. What does Paul say will happen to those peole who do not have sound doctrine and lead others astray with their false teachings (see verses 10–11)?

_____

_____

_____

_____

_____

REVIEWING THE STORY

John picks up in his second letter where his first one left off. He reiterates his plea for believers to love one another. He points out that love is a natural outgrowth of living according to God's commandments. Yet he encourages his readers to withhold godly love and hospitality from a certain group of people who were teaching that Jesus was not truly human but only divine. The threat these false teachers posed was so great that John warned even associating with them could jeopardize their heavenly rewards.

9. What caused John to rejoice (see 2 John 1:4)?

_____

_____

_____

10. What does John say represents our love for God (see 2 John 1:6)?

_____

_____

_____

_____

11. How does John refer to the false teachers in the church
(see 2 John 1:7–8)?

_____

_____

_____

_____

_____

_____

12. What does John say about the person who does not follow sound
doctrine (see 2 John 1:9)?

_____

_____

_____

_____

_____

_____

APPLYING THE MESSAGE

13. What does "walking in truth" look like in your life?

_____

_____

_____

_____

_____

_____

14. How can you stay vigilant against those who might lead you away from Christ?

_____

_____

_____

_____

REFLECTING ON THE MEANING

"Deceivers" caused problems in the early church, and they still cause problems for believers today. People who twist God's Word for their own gain—or whose "walk" doesn't match their "talk"—cause others to doubt the sincerity of all believers. When the deceivers' actions are publicly exposed, they make us all susceptible to accusations of hypocrisy.

The best way for sincere believers to combat the influence of deceivers is to be a living example of what it means to follow Christ. We need to walk in truth in everything we do—especially when it's hard to do. We need to recognize that our obedience to God impacts more than just our own lives. We need to understand that our actions create ripple effects that extend far beyond our own limited vision of a situation.

Think about the people in your world—those outside the church. How might your obedience or disobedience to God influence them? What happens when they see the choices you make in your daily life? Does it confirm the world's suspicions that Christians are just a bunch of hypocrites? Or does it cause them to rethink this view of God's people?

As John writes in his second letter, the secret to living a life that honors God is to love others, abide in God's truth, and be consistent in obeying Christ in the big things and small. In the long run, one grand gesture of obedience will not have nearly the impact of countless small ones . . . because the reality is that few things go unnoticed. Someone is always watching us, whether we realize it or not. And when people catch us faithfully obeying the Lord whom we claim to love, they will see the truth in our words.

JOURNALING YOUR RESPONSE

What is one thing you can demonstrate to another person to help them "walk the walk"?

LIVING FOR OTHERS

3 John 1:1–14

GETTING STARTED

In what ways have you been blessed by acts of hospitality?

_____

_____

_____

_____

_____

_____

_____

_____

_____

_____

_____

_____

_____

_____

SETTING THE STAGE

The apostle John's final letter offers a contrast to what he wrote in his second letter. In that epistle, John instructed believers to *not* entertain or even associate with the travelling teachers who were promoting a false doctrine of Christ. But in his third letter, John instructs believers to show hospitality to those travelling teachers who are promoting God's truth.

The letter is addressed to an elder in the church named Gaius, a man whose reputation for selflessly serving others evidently preceded him. Gaius's ministry niche was hospitality and encouragement. He worked behind the scenes to prepare, support, and empower others to serve God. And God used Gaius's work to accomplish extraordinary things.

Our modern culture emphasizes building one's brand, becoming an influencer, and going viral. The cult of celebrity looms large. The unspoken rule is that if you want to do great things, other people need to consider you to be great. This creates a difficult dynamic for believers, who are all parts of one body. While it is true that God calls some people to serve on the "front lines" as pastors and teachers, their role is no more important than anyone else's in the body of Christ. In fact, their roles would not be possible if it weren't for others.

John's final letter is an encouragement for everyone who works behind the scenes to ensure that God's work gets done. It is for the "others" whose actions rarely get noticed—and an important reminder that everyone is essential in the body of Christ. For Gaius represents all Christians who selflessly contribute to God's work in this world.

EXPLORING THE TEXT

Gaius Commended for Generosity (3 John 1:1–8)

[1] The Elder,

To the beloved Gaius, whom I love in truth:

[2] Beloved, I pray that you may prosper in all things and be in health, just as your soul prospers. [3] For I rejoiced greatly when brethren came and testified of the truth that is in you, just as you walk in the truth. [4] I have no greater joy than to hear that my children walk in truth.

⁵ Beloved, you do faithfully whatever you do for the brethren and for strangers, ⁶ who have borne witness of your love before the church. If you send them forward on their journey in a manner worthy of God, you will do well, ⁷ because they went forth for His name's sake, taking nothing from the Gentiles. ⁸ We therefore ought to receive such, that we may become fellow workers for the truth.

---

1. John opens by expressing his deep love and his prayers for Gaius, a fellow believer in Christ. What reports about Gaius caused John to rejoice greatly (see verses 1–4)?

_____

_____

_____

2. John had also received reports about Gaius's acts of service to both those inside and outside the church. What are some of these acts that John notes (see verses 5–8)?

_____

_____

_____

_____

_____

Farewell Greeting (3 John 1:9–14)

⁹ I wrote to the church, but Diotrephes, who loves to have the pre-eminence among them, does not receive us. ¹⁰ Therefore, if I come, I will call to mind his deeds which he does, prating against us with malicious words. And not content with that, he himself does not receive the brethren, and forbids those who wish to, putting them out of the church.

¹¹ Beloved, do not imitate what is evil, but what is good. He who does good is of God, but he who does evil has not seen God.

¹² Demetrius has a good testimony from all, and from the truth itself. And we also bear witness, and you know that our testimony is true.

¹³ I had many things to write, but I do not wish to write to you with pen and ink; ¹⁴ but I hope to see you shortly, and we shall speak face to face.

Peace to you. Our friends greet you. Greet the friends by name.

---

3. Unfortunately, not everyone in the church was as faithful and selfless as Gaius. John had written an earlier letter that apparently was destroyed by a church leader named Diotrephes. What other offenses had Diotrephes committed (see verses 9–10)?

_____

_____

_____

_____

_____

4. John writes that "he who does good is of God, but he who does evil has not seen God" (verse 11). Diotrephes was an example of a person who had done much evil. What does John say that Demetrius, another member of the church, had done (see verses 11–12)?

_____

_____

_____

_____

_____

Going Deeper

In this short letter, John summarizes the report he heard about Gaius—namely, that he had sent Christian ministers on their way "in a manner worthy of God." The implication is that Gaius offered both respect and financial support. In other words, *he served others well*. Gaius demonstrated the kind of service that both Peter and James talk about in their letters.

Serving for God's Glory (1 Peter 4:7–11)

7 But the end of all things is at hand; therefore be serious and watchful in your prayers. 8 And above all things have fervent love for one another, for "love will cover a multitude of sins." 9 Be hospitable to one another without grumbling. 10 As each one has received a gift, minister it to one another, as good stewards of the manifold grace of God. 11 If anyone speaks, let him speak as the oracles of God. If anyone ministers, let him do it as with the ability which God supplies, that in all things God may be glorified through Jesus Christ, to whom belong the glory and the dominion forever and ever. Amen.

5. The apostle Peter issues a warning that the "end of all things is at hand." His readers would have understood that he was referring to the time of Jesus' return and the day of judgment. How does this add urgency to his request for believers to love one another (see verses 7–8)?

6. Peter emphasizes not only showing hospitality but also having a good attitude when serving others. How does he instruct believers to use their God-given gifts (see verses 9–11)?

_____

_____

_____

_____

_____

Faith Without Works Is Dead (James 2:14–18)

¹⁴ What does it profit, my brethren, if someone says he has faith but does not have works? Can faith save him? ¹⁵ If a brother or sister is naked and destitute of daily food, ¹⁶ and one of you says to them, "Depart in peace, be warmed and filled," but you do not give them the things which are needed for the body, what does it profit? ¹⁷ Thus also faith by itself, if it does not have works, is dead.

¹⁸ But someone will say, "You have faith, and I have works." Show me your faith without your works, and I will show you my faith by my works.

7. James writes there is actually no _profit_—no benefit or advantage— if we say we have faith in Christ but do not live out our faith through our actions. What example does he cite to show how important it is to back up our words with good deeds (see verses 14–16).

_____

_____

_____

_____

_____

8. James considers a faith that is devoid of serving others in love to be a *dead* faith. What argument does he anticipate to this statement? How does he respond (see verses 17–18)?

_____

_____

_____

_____

REVIEWING THE STORY

John addresses his third letter to a believer named Gaius, who had made a name for himself as an equipper and encourager of God's people. Gaius opened his home to ministers and missionaries, supplied for their needs, and prepared them for their work. In extending this hospitality, Gaius became a part of their work. In contrast, a man named Diotrephes in the same church was withholding hospitality in an effort to establish control. John duly commends Gaius for his valuable ministry and condemns Diotrephes for his wickedness.

9. What gave John his greatest joy (see 3 John 1:4)?

_____

_____

_____

_____

10. What happens when we receive and support God's workers (see 3 John 1:8)?

_____

_____

_____

_____

11. Why was John planning to confront Diotrephes
(see 3 John 1:9–10)?

12. What was John's advice to his readers after calling out the actions
of Gaius and Diotrephes (see 3 John 1:11)?

APPLYING THE MESSAGE

13. What kind of support and encouragement would help you as you
do God's work?

14. How can you provide that kind of support and encouragement
to others?

REFLECTING ON THE MEANING

According to John's words in this letter, four things happen when we live selflessly, as Gaius did. *First, we prosper in our own souls* (see 3 John 1:2). Most of the work done in churches is done behind the scenes, where hardly anyone sees what is accomplished but God. There is little glory or recognition in it. But God sees the selflessness in such work and blesses it. Gaius could testify to that fact. He reached out to prosper others and prospered his own soul in the process.

Second, we proclaim the truth (see 3 John 1:5–6). Gaius opened his home to strangers and missionaries. In doing so, he became a part of the "evangelism process." He provided a stable base of operation for the missionaries who stayed in his home so they could accomplish the work of spreading the gospel. He provided a living example of what it looks like to be in the body of Christ to the strangers who stayed with him. In the same way, when we support the work of the church, we participate in the mission of the church.

Third, we participate in the ministry of others (see 3 John 1:8). Not all of us are called by God to be missionaries in foreign lands or preachers in our communities. Most of us will be called to hold down a secular job, stay in one place, and carry out the routine duties of life. But we *are* all called to support those in the ministry to one degree or another. When we do this, we make ourselves allies of the truth and participate in the results of that ministry.

Fourth, we please the Lord (see 3 John 1:11). Sometimes, we need a little pat on the back from Scripture. When we read the Word of God, we discover that God frequently and figuratively puts His arm around us and says, "You do well. You do faithfully. You do good." We can know that when we serve as Jesus served, God is pleased with our actions.

Our acts of service likely won't make us stand out in the world. But we can be assured that God sees our acts. As Jesus said, "When you do a charitable deed, do not let your left hand know what your right hand is doing, that your charitable deed may be in secret; and your Father who sees in secret will Himself reward you openly" (Matthew 6:3–4).

JOURNALING YOUR RESPONSE

How are you supporting those in ministry through your acts of service?

CONTENDING FOR THE FAITH

Jude 1:1–25

GETTING STARTED

How do you stay grounded in God's truth so you can respond to those who oppose it?

_____

_____

_____

_____

_____

_____

_____

_____

_____

_____

SETTING THE STAGE

Jude, the writer of the penultimate book of the Bible, has an interesting backstory. Like James, he was likely the half-brother of Jesus. He grew up in the same family as the Messiah. The years of mysterious silence that marked Jesus' life from his visit to the Temple in Jerusalem at age twelve (see Luke 2:41–50) to His baptism by John in the Jordan River (see 3:21–22) were no mystery to Jude. He had a younger sibling's perspective on all of it. Yet, apparently, Jude didn't recognize Jesus for who He truly was until after Jesus' death and resurrection (see John 7:5).

The name *Jude* is a translation of the Hebrew name *Judah* and can also be rendered *Judas*. We find this form of the name in the two places in the Gospels where Jude/Judas is listed as being of member of Jesus' human family (see Matthew 13:55; Mark 6:3). Beyond these two references, the only other definitive information we have about Jude is what we find in his letter. And what we find there is a man who cared deeply about God's truth and His church.

Just as the disciple John did with his second letter, Jude wrote his letter to make believers aware of certain deceivers in the church. Apparently, these false teachers had disguised their true purposes and were making inroads into people's lives. Jude is forthright in discussing his feelings about these individuals. He reminds his readers of how God dealt with similar acts of disobedience in the past, leaving no doubt that these teachers will face God's judgment.

The problem of false teaching has only grown since Jude wrote this letter. Social media offers a platform to anyone who desires to alter Christian truths—and many people today choose to take advantage of it. This is one reason why Jude's words still resonate 2,000 years after they were written. The letter of Jude gives us marching orders for how to respond to these manipulations.

EXPLORING THE TEXT

Contend for the Faith (Jude 1:1–11)

¹ Jude, a bondservant of Jesus Christ, and brother of James, to those who are called, sanctified by God the Father, and preserved in Jesus Christ:

² Mercy, peace, and love be multiplied to you.

³ Beloved, while I was very diligent to write to you concerning our common salvation, I found it necessary to write to you exhorting you to contend earnestly for the faith which was once for all delivered to the saints. ⁴ For certain men have crept in unnoticed, who long ago were marked out for this condemnation, ungodly men, who turn the grace of our God into lewdness and deny the only Lord God and our Lord Jesus Christ.

⁵ But I want to remind you, though you once knew this, that the Lord, having saved the people out of the land of Egypt, afterward destroyed those who did not believe. ⁶ And the angels who did not keep their proper domain, but left their own abode, He has reserved in everlasting chains under darkness for the judgment of the great day; ⁷ as Sodom and Gomorrah, and the cities around them in a similar manner to these, having given themselves over to sexual immorality and gone after strange flesh, are set forth as an example, suffering the vengeance of eternal fire.

⁸ Likewise also these dreamers defile the flesh, reject authority, and speak evil of dignitaries. ⁹ Yet Michael the archangel, in contending with the devil, when he disputed about the body of Moses, dared not bring against him a reviling accusation, but said, "The Lord rebuke you!" ¹⁰ But these speak evil of whatever they do not know; and whatever they know naturally, like brute beasts, in these things they corrupt themselves. ¹¹ Woe to them! For they have gone in the way of Cain, have run greedily in the error of Balaam for profit, and perished in the rebellion of Korah.

---

1. Jude opens by identifying himself as "a bondservant of Jesus Christ" and brother of James, and then immediately stresses the purpose of his letter. Interestingly, he had initially intended to write to this group of believers about salvation, but disturbing news had compelled him to change his topic. What was this crisis (see verses 1–4)?

_____

_____

_____

_____

_____

_____

_____

2. Jude uses the phrase "though you once knew this" in verse 5 to remind his readers of the teachings of Jesus, the apostles, and the testimony of Scripture regarding those who defy God. What do his examples all have in common (see verses 5–11)?

_____

_____

_____

_____

_____

Maintain Your Life with God (Jude 1:12–25)

¹² These are spots in your love feasts, while they feast with you without fear, serving only themselves. They are clouds without water, carried about by the winds; late autumn trees without fruit, twice dead, pulled up by the roots; ¹³ raging waves of the sea, foaming up their own shame; wandering stars for whom is reserved the blackness of darkness forever.

¹⁴ Now Enoch, the seventh from Adam, prophesied about these men also, saying, "Behold, the Lord comes with ten thousands of His

saints, [15] to execute judgment on all, to convict all who are ungodly among them of all their ungodly deeds which they have committed in an ungodly way, and of all the harsh things which ungodly sinners have spoken against Him."

[16] These are grumblers, complainers, walking according to their own lusts; and they mouth great swelling words, flattering people to gain advantage. [17] But you, beloved, remember the words which were spoken before by the apostles of our Lord Jesus Christ: [18] how they told you that there would be mockers in the last time who would walk according to their own ungodly lusts. [19] These are sensual persons, who cause divisions, not having the Spirit.

[20] But you, beloved, building yourselves up on your most holy faith, praying in the Holy Spirit, [21] keep yourselves in the love of God, looking for the mercy of our Lord Jesus Christ unto eternal life.

[22] And on some have compassion, making a distinction; [23] but others save with fear, pulling them out of the fire, hating even the garment defiled by the flesh.

[24] Now to Him who is able to keep you from stumbling,
And to present you faultless
Before the presence of His glory with exceeding joy,
[25] To God our Savior,
Who alone is wise,
Be glory and majesty,
Dominion and power,
Both now and forever.
Amen.

---

3. Jude draws on a number of metaphors in these verses to describe the false teachers and the negative impact that they were having on the Christian community. He then quotes from an ancient Hebrew text called the Book of Enoch. How would Enoch's prophecy have served

as a warning to the false teachers who posed such a problem for Jude's
readers (see verses 14–15)?

_____

_____

_____

_____

_____

4. Jude concludes his short but pointed letter with a few instructions
and a prayer. What does he advise the believers to do to protect
themselves against false teachings? What does he say in his prayer that
God will do for them (see verses 20–25)?

_____

_____

_____

_____

GOING DEEPER

Jude draws on a number of examples from the Old Testament to explain
how God punishes those who twist His truths and deceive others. One
story is found in Exodus, when the Israelites were camped at the foot of
Mount Sinai. Moses had ascended the mountain to be with the Lord,
and when he delayed in coming down, the people despaired. So Aaron,
Moses' brother, allowed them to create a golden calf to worship. God was
not pleased with their actions.

Who Is on the Lord's Side? (Exodus 32:25–29)

> 25 Now when Moses saw that the people were unrestrained (for
> Aaron had not restrained them, to their shame among their enemies),

²⁶ then Moses stood in the entrance of the camp, and said, "Whoever is on the LORD's side—come to me!" And all the sons of Levi gathered themselves together to him. ²⁷ And he said to them, "Thus says the LORD God of Israel: 'Let every man put his sword on his side, and go in and out from entrance to entrance throughout the camp, and let every man kill his brother, every man his companion, and every man his neighbor.' " ²⁸ So the sons of Levi did according to the word of Moses. And about three thousand men of the people fell that day. ²⁹ Then Moses said, "Consecrate yourselves today to the LORD, that He may bestow on you a blessing this day, for every man has opposed his son and his brother."

5. When Moses finally descended the mountain after forty days, he found the people worshiping a calf made of gold they had created themselves. What role did Aaron play in this? What was Moses' immediate instruction (see verses 25–26)?

_____

_____

_____

_____

_____

6. What were the consequences of the people's actions? What was Moses' final instruction to them on this day (see verses 27–29)?

_____

_____

_____

_____

_____

_____

Jude closes his letter with a benediction that urges the believers to contend for the faith. His words are reminiscent of the benediction that Paul uses to conclude the first half of Ephesians. In that passage, Paul urges the believers to also be strengthened in the faith.

Strengthened Through the Spirit (Ephesians 3:14–21)

¹⁴ For this reason I bow my knees to the Father of our Lord Jesus Christ, ¹⁵ from whom the whole family in heaven and earth is named, ¹⁶ that He would grant you, according to the riches of His glory, to be strengthened with might through His Spirit in the inner man, ¹⁷ that Christ may dwell in your hearts through faith; that you, being rooted and grounded in love, ¹⁸ may be able to comprehend with all the saints what is the width and length and depth and height— ¹⁹ to know the love of Christ which passes knowledge; that you may be filled with all the fullness of God.

²⁰ Now to Him who is able to do exceedingly abundantly above all that we ask or think, according to the power that works in us, ²¹ to Him be glory in the church by Christ Jesus to all generations, forever and ever. Amen.

7. The word that is translated as *dwell* in verse 17 suggests settling in at home. What does Christ's dwelling in our hearts allow us to do (see verses 14–19)?

8. Paul's doxology, or praise, to God marks the end of the first half of the book of Ephesians. What does Paul want his readers to remember at this point (see verses 20–21)?

_____

_____

_____

_____

REVIEWING THE STORY

The book of Jude is a call to action. From his vantage point as an elder of the Christian faith, Jude could spot the subtle influences of false teachers. The people to whom he was writing either could not spot them or chose not to do anything about them. Their live-and-let-live attitude threatened to destroy the church. So Jude issued an urgent call for them to fight for the truth, reminding them of how God punished disobedience in the past. Jude revealed the false teachers for who and what they were and urged believers not to give them an audience.

9. What does Jude say about the recipients of his letter (see Jude 1:1)?

_____

_____

_____

10. What acts were "certain men" in the congregation doing (see Jude 1:4)?

_____

_____

_____

_____

11. What does Jude say about the words that these men spoke (see Jude 1:10)?

_____

_____

_____

_____

12. What verbal clues did these teachers give that revealed what their hearts were really like (see Jude 1:16)?

_____

_____

_____

_____

APPLYING THE MESSAGE

13. When are times that God sent people into your life to guide you back to His truth?

_____

_____

_____

_____

14. When are times that God has used you to guide others back to the truth?

_____

_____

_____

_____

Reflecting on the Meaning

Jude wrote his letter with a sense of urgency. He needed to confront the issue of false teaching immediately, for he knew that unsound doctrine is like an invasive plant species. If given the chance to take root, it will spread, choke out truthful teaching, and be difficult to eliminate. So, in this brief letter, Jude provides several strategies on combating false teachings.

First, *be an expert in what God's Word actually says.* Jude instructs, "[Build] yourselves up on your most holy faith" (1:20). Work to understand the *why* and *how* of Scripture, in addition to the *who, what,* and *when.* Draw on trustworthy sources to fill in your comprehension gaps. "Contend earnestly" in your study so that alarm bells go off in your head when you hear something that doesn't sound right.

Second, *maintain your relationship with God.* Jude states, "Keep yourselves in the love of God" (verse 21). Make it a point to spend time with God each day so that you can hear the voice of the Holy Spirit speaking into your life. As you grow closer to God and develop in spiritual maturity, you will find it easier to spot the subtle deceptions of the enemy and call them out for the lies they represent.

Third, *lovingly confront people about things that don't sound right to you.* Jude advises, "On some have compassion, making a distinction; but others save with fear, pulling them out of the fire, hating even the garment defiled by the flesh" (verses 22–23). Ask clarifying questions to make sure that you are properly understanding what the person is saying. Have compassion on those who are being deceived and lovingly guide them back to the truth of the gospel. But also confront those who are distorting God's truth. In this way you might pull them "out of the fire" and save them from unfortunate consequences.

We all need to take Jude's words to heart whenever we hear a message that runs contrary to the gospel. This is not only for our own benefit but for the benefit of our fellow brothers and sisters in Christ. We need to remember that the church is the *body* of Christ, and when one member suffers—or is deceived—the whole community suffers.

JOURNALING YOUR RESPONSE

How can you better prepare yourself to contend for the faith?

LEADER'S GUIDE

Thank you for choosing to lead your group through this study from Dr. David Jeremiah on *The Letters of 1, 2, 3 John and Jude*. Being a group leader has its own rewards, and it is our prayer that your walk with the Lord will deepen through this experience. During the twelve lessons in this study, you and your group will read passages from 1, 2, 3 John and Jude, explore key themes in the letter based on teachings from Dr. Jeremiah, and review questions that will encourage group discussion. There are multiple components in this section that can help you structure your lessons and discussion time, so please be sure to read and consider each one.

Before You Begin

Before your first meeting, make sure you and your group are well versed with the content of the lesson. Group members should have their own copy of *The Letters of 1, 2, 3 John and Jude* study guide prior to the first meeting so they can follow along and record their answers, thoughts, and insights. After the first week, you may wish to assign the study guide lesson as homework prior to the group meeting and then use the meeting time to discuss the content in the lesson.

To ensure everyone has a chance to participate in the discussion, the ideal size for a group is around eight to ten people. If there are more than ten people, break up the bigger group into smaller subgroups. Make sure the members are committed to participating each week, as this will help create stability and help you better prepare the structure of the meeting.

At the beginning of each week's study, start with the opening Getting Started question to introduce the topic you will be discussing. The members should answer briefly, as the goal is just for them to have an idea of the subject in their minds as you go over the lesson. This will allow the members to become engaged and ready to interact with the rest of the group.

After reviewing the lesson, try to initiate a free-flowing discussion. Invite group members to bring questions and insights they may have discovered to the next meeting, especially if they were unsure of the meaning of some parts of the lesson. Be prepared to discuss how biblical truth applies to the world we live in today.

WEEKLY PREPARATION

As the group leader, here are a few things that you can do to prepare for each meeting:

- *Be thoroughly familiar with the material in the lesson.* Make sure that you understand the content of each lesson so you know how to structure the group time and are prepared to lead the group discussion.

- *Decide, ahead of time, which questions you want to discuss.* Depending on how much time you have each week, you may not be able to reflect on every question. Select specific questions that you feel will evoke the best discussion.

- *Take prayer requests.* At the end of your discussion, take prayer requests from your group members and then pray for one another.

STRUCTURING THE DISCUSSION TIME

There are several ways to structure the duration of the study. You can choose to cover each lesson individually, for a total of twelve weeks of group meetings, or you can combine two lessons together per week, for a total of six weeks of group meetings. The following charts illustrate these options:

TWELVE-WEEK FORMAT

Week	Lessons Covered	Reading
1	The Fullness of Joy	1 John 1:1–10
2	Trust and Obey	1 John 2:1–14
3	Loving the World	1 John 2:15–29
4	We Shall Be Like Him!	1 John 3:1–12
5	The Problem with Hate	1 John 3:13–24
6	Loving God—Loving Each Other	1 John 4:1–11
7	Casting Out Fear	1 John 4:12–21
8	Commandment Keepers	1 John 5:1–10
9	Assurance of Salvation	1 John 5:11–21
10	Walking the Walk	2 John 1:1–13
11	Living for Others	3 John 1:1–14
12	Contending for the Faith	Jude 1:1–25

SIX-WEEK FORMAT

Week	Lessons Covered	Reading
1	The Fullness of Joy / Trust and Obey	1 John 1:1–14
2	Loving the World / We Shall Be Like Him!	1 John 2:15–3:12
3	The Problem with Hate / Loving God—Loving Each Other	1 John 3:13–4:11
4	Casting Out Fear / Commandment Keepers	1 John 4:12–5:10
5	Assurance of Salvation / Walking the Walk	1 John 5:11–2 John 1:13
6	Living for Others / Contending for the Faith	3 John 1:1–Jude 1:25

In regard to organizing your time when planning your group Bible study, the following two schedules, for sixty minutes and ninety minutes, can give you a structure for the lesson:

Section	60 Minutes	90 Minutes
Welcome: Members arrive and get settled	5 minutes	10 minutes
Getting Started Question: Prepares the group for interacting with one another	10 minutes	10 minutes
Message: Review the lesson	15 minutes	25 minutes
Discussion: Discuss questions in the lesson	25 minutes	35 minutes
Review and Prayer: Review the key points of the lesson and have a closing time of prayer	5 minutes	10 minutes

As the group leader, it is up to you to keep track of the time and keep things moving according to your schedule. If your group is having a good discussion, don't feel the need to stop and move on to the next question. Remember, the purpose is to pull together ideas and share unique insights on the lesson. Encourage everyone to participate, but don't be concerned if certain group members are more quiet. They may just be internally reflecting on the questions and need time to process their ideas before they can share them.

GROUP DYNAMICS

Leading a group study can be a rewarding experience for you and your group members—but that doesn't mean there won't be challenges. Certain members may feel uncomfortable discussing topics that they consider very personal and might be afraid of being called on. Some members might have disagreements on specific issues. To help prevent these scenarios, consider the following ground rules:

- If someone has a question that may seem off topic, suggest that it be discussed at another time, or ask the group if they are okay with addressing that topic.

- If someone asks a question you don't know the answer to, confess that you don't know and move on. If you feel comfortable, invite other group members to give their opinions or share their comments based on personal experience.

- If you feel like a couple of people are talking much more than others, direct questions to people who may not have shared yet. You could even ask the more dominating members to help draw out the quiet ones.

- When there is a disagreement, encourage the group members to process the matter in love. Invite members from opposing sides to evaluate their opinions and consider the ideas of the other members. Lead the group through Scripture that addresses the topic, and look for common ground.

When issues arise, encourage your group to think of Scripture: "Love one another" (John 13:34), "If it is possible, as much as depends on you, live peaceably with all men" (Romans 12:18), and, "Be swift to hear, slow to speak, slow to wrath" (James 1:19).

ABOUT

Dr. David Jeremiah and Turning Point

Dr. David Jeremiah is the founder of Turning Point, a ministry committed to providing Christians with sound Bible teaching relevant to today's changing times through radio and television broadcasts, audio series, books, and live events. Dr. Jeremiah's teaching on topics such as family, prayer, worship, angels, and biblical prophecy forms the foundation of Turning Point.

David and his wife, Donna, reside in El Cajon, California, where he serves as the senior pastor of Shadow Mountain Community Church. David and Donna have four children and twelve grandchildren.

In 1982, Dr. Jeremiah brought the same solid teaching to San Diego television that he shares weekly with his congregation. Shortly thereafter, Turning Point expanded its ministry to radio. Dr. Jeremiah's inspiring messages can now be heard worldwide on radio, television, and the internet.

Because Dr. Jeremiah desires to know his listening audience, he travels nationwide holding ministry rallies and spiritual enrichment conferences that touch the hearts and lives of many people. According to Dr. Jeremiah, "At some point in time, everyone reaches a turning point; and for every person, that moment is unique, an experience to hold onto forever. There's so much changing in today's world that sometimes it's difficult to choose the right path. Turning Point offers people an understanding of God's Word and seeks to make a difference in their lives."

Dr. Jeremiah has authored numerous books, including *Escape the Coming Night* (Revelation), *The Handwriting on the Wall* (Daniel), *Overcoming Loneliness, What in the World Is Going On?, The Coming Economic Armageddon, I Never Thought I'd See the Day!, God Loves You: He Always Has—He Always Will, Agents of the Apocalypse, Agents of Babylon, People Are Asking . . . Is This the End?, A Life Beyond Amazing, Overcomer, The Book of Signs, Everything You Need, Forward,* and *Where Do We Go from Here?*

New Bible Study Series
from Dr. David Jeremiah

The Jeremiah Bible Study Series captures Dr. David Jeremiah's forty-plus years of commitment to teaching the whole Word of God. Each volume contains twelve lessons for individuals and groups to explore what the Bible says, what it meant to the people at the time it was written, and what it means to us today. Out of his lifelong ministry of *delivering the unchanging Word of God to an ever-changing world*, Dr. Jeremiah has written this Bible-strong study series focused not on causes, current events, or politics, but on the solid truth of Scripture.

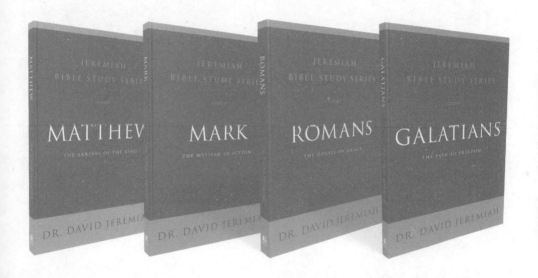

9780310091493	Matthew	9780310097488	2 Corinthians
9780310091516	Mark	9780310091660	Galatians
9780310091530	Luke	9780310091684	Ephesians
9780310091554	John	9780310091707	Philippians
9780310091608	Acts	9780310091721	Colossians and Philemon
9780310091622	Romans	9780310091745	1 & 2 Thessalonians
9780310091646	1 Corinthians	9780310091769	1 & 2 Timothy and Titus

Available now at your favorite bookstore.

HarperChristian Resources